Digital
Design
in *Action*

Digital
Design
in
Action

Digital Design
in *Action*

Creative Solutions for Designers

Chris Jackson

Nancy Ciolek

CRC Press
Taylor & Francis Group
Boca Raton London New York

CRC Press is an imprint of the
Taylor & Francis Group, an **informa** business

A CHAPMAN & HALL BOOK

CRC Press
Taylor & Francis Group
6000 Broken Sound Parkway NW, Suite 300
Boca Raton, FL 33487-2742

© 2017 by FocalPress/CRC Press
CRC Press is an imprint of Taylor & Francis Group, an Informa business

No claim to original U.S. Government works

Printed and bound in India by Replika Press Pvt. Ltd.

Printed on acid-free paper
Version Date: 20161010

International Standard Book Number-13: 978-1-138-83173-5 (Paperback) 978-1-138-62876-2 (Hardback)

**Visit the Taylor & Francis Web site at
http://www.taylorandfrancis.com**

**and the CRC Press Web site at
http://www.crcpress.com**

Table of Contents

Introduction

Welcome to *Digital Design in Action*. Digital design is not just about making things look visually attractive on the screen. It encompasses research, planning, presentation, and programming. You are about to take a journey that explores practical and creative designs for mobile apps, electronic publications (EPUBs), web, visual presentations, and PDF documents.

This Introduction discusses the overall structure of the book and its primary audience, artists and designers.

What Is This Book About?

Digital Design in Action explores practical and creative designs for mobile apps, EPUBs, web, visual presentations, and PDF documents. With the Adobe Creative Cloud, artists and designers can develop and implement layouts that go beyond print to include web, tablets, and mobile devices. Written for designers, *Digital Design in Action*, deconstructs creative design solutions, providing valuable insights into the design process and methodologies used to deploy layouts for multiple output.

Each chapter balances the design aspects with related techniques. This includes composition and layout, visual hierarchy, typography, responsive design, media integration, and interactivity. Using the latest digital publishing tools and the project-based design techniques outlined in this book, a reader will be able to design their visual solutions for a variety of digital output.

The book is designed to walk the reader through project-based case studies that effectively enhance their design skills. Each chapter contains a unique project exercise that offers timesaving practical tips and hands-on design techniques. It also discusses adding interactivity to enhance audience participation. The last section discusses usability testing for digital design.

Each exercise provides step-by-step instructions and tips for the reader to use in conceptualizing and visualizing creative solutions for their own digital design projects. What differentiates this book from similar Focal Press books is that readers will view or build professional world examples in each chapter and, as a result, learn how to effectively design using Adobe software through the project implementations rather than reading chapters that only explain software interfaces and tools. Practical application is the best way to learn and understand how to design, develop, and deploy for digital output.

Chapter projects are geared to simulate actual client-work/practical solutions that artists and designers have used in the industry. Individual projects for each chapter include:

- Designing a Visual Presentation and Integrating Media
- Prototyping a Functional User Interface Design
- Exploring Responsive Layouts for Web Design
- Animating a Parallax Scroll for a Web Page
- Designing an EPUB Children's Book
- Developing an Interactive PDF Form
- Illustrating a Visual Storyboard for an Animated Short

Who Should Read This Book?

The primary audience for this book is artists and designers. These readers can be professionals in the workforce, students, educators, or anyone interested in creatively designing, developing, and deploying digital solutions. They should have a basic working knowledge of Adobe software (InDesign, Illustrator, Photoshop, Acrobat, and Dreamweaver). The chapter exercises teach readers how to think creatively and get excited about pushing their design skills to the next level.

Book Layout Conventions

To help you get the most out of this book, let's look at the layout conventions used in the chapters.

- Words in **bold** within the main text refer to keywords, names of files, and folders.

- Menu selections are presented like this: **File > Place**.

- Supplemental information to the text that sheds light on a procedure or offers miscellaneous options available to you appear in a side column.

Icons are used throughout the book. Here is a brief explanation of what they are and what they mean.

- **Download Source Files:** The source files for this book are available to readers at **www.routledge.com/cw/Jackson**

- **Book Resources:** Supplemental book resources.

- **Online Resources:** Supplemental online resources.

All of the chapter exercise files are provided to readers at the following URL: *www.routledge.com/cw/Jackson*. Chapter exercises have their own compressed (zip) file. Inside each folder you will find the material needed to complete each exercise. Completed versions for every exercise are provided.

All of the material inside this book and accompanying digital files are copyright protected. They are included only for your learning and experimentation. Please respect the copyright. We encourage you to use your own artwork and experiment with each exercise. This is not an exact science. The specific values given in this book are suggestions. If you want to experiment, by all means, do so. That is the best way to learn.

About the Authors

Chris Jackson is a computer graphics designer, professor, and graduate director of the MFA Visual Communication Design program at the Rochester Institute of Technology (RIT). Before joining the RIT faculty, Chris was a new media designer with Eastman KODAK Company, creating and delivering online instructional training via the Web and CD-ROM. He continues to be an animator, designer, developer, and consultant for global corporations. He lectures and conducts workshops relating to interactive design and motion graphics.

Chris's professional work has received over 25 distinguished national and international awards for online communication. His areas of research include user experience design, 2D character animation, digital storytelling, and interactive design for children. Chris continues to publish and present his research and professional work at Adobe MAX, ACM SIGGRAPH, and the Society for Technical Communication (STC). Chris is the author of *After Effects and CINEMA 4D Lite* (Focal Press, September 2014), *Flash + After Effects* (Focal Press, August 2010), *Flash Cinematic Techniques* (Focal Press, January 2010), and co-author of *Flash 3D: Animation, Interactivity and Games* (Focal Press, October 2006).

Nancy Ciolek is a designer and professor at the Rochester Institute of Technology, former chair of the Graphic Design Department, and administrative chair of the School of Design. Previously, Nancy worked for James Bare Design and St. Mary of the Woods College, before joining the faculty at RIT. Nancy continues to be active in the profession through freelance and consulting work, including service as a conference program reviewer, invited guest educator and speaker, and design consulting for businesses, state education departments, and non-profit organizations.

Nancy has more than 30 years of experience in graphic design. She has presented at conferences including SIGGRAPH, UCDA, Kern Conference, TypeCon, and USG Teaching & Learning Conference. Nancy also attends Adobe MAX to keep current on the changing software landscape as related to design. Her design, consulting, and training freelance work includes work for RIT Press, Dotted Lines Press, SIGGRAPH Education Committee, Idea Connection Systems, and many other clients. Nancy has been published in conference proceedings for SIGGRAPH, in the St. James Press book *Contemporary Masterworks*, and a white paper for an online conference for IDS Publishing/Media.

For Instructors

Digital Design in Action provides hands-on exercises that clearly demonstrate core features in Adobe products. As instructors, we know you appreciate the hard work and effort that goes into creating lessons and examples for your courses. We hope you find the information and exercises useful and can adapt them for your own classes.

All that we ask is for your help and cooperation in protecting the copyright of this book. If an instructor or student distributes copies of the source files to anyone who has not purchased the book, they are violating the copyright protection. Reproducing pages from this book or duplicating any part of the source files is also a copyright infringement. If you own the book, you can adapt the exercises using your own footage and artwork without infringing the copyright. Thank you for your cooperation!

Credits

We would like to thank the following people for their contributions to this book:

- Steve Wilson, *Business Woman*, Chapter 1
  www.flickr.com/photos/125303894@N06/14387365942/

- Lisa Zahra, *DEAAF images and text,* Chapter 2

- Vincent Petaccio, *Water Faucet*, Chapter 2
  www.freeimages.com/photo/full-1171768

- Craig Young, *Coins 4*, Chapter 2
  www.freeimages.com/photo/coins-4-1459115

- *App wireframes and prototype*, Ninglin Jiang, *Seneca Park Zoo Info Guide and Event Planner*, Chapter 3 Case Study

- *App wireframes*, Yue Liu, *Roc Doc App*, Chapter 3

- *Preliminary app sketches,* Kaige Liu, *Schedule It! App*, Chapter 3

- *App wireframes,* Tejal Sampat, *timeOut App*, Chapter 3
  App wireframes, Tejal Sampat, *timeOut App*, Chapter 4 Case Study

- Zhaolifang, *Dinosaur Bones Vectors*, Chapter 8
  www.vecteezy.com/vector-art/83009-dinosaur-bones-vectors

- Stay Media Productions, *Cityscape at Night,* Chapter 9
  illustration courtesy of iStockphoto, Image# 1564950

- Belkarus, *Cowboy in the Dusk,* Chapter 9
  illustration courtesy of iStockphoto, Image# 9481995

- *App wireframes and prototype*, Jordan Reading,
  ROC DOX App, Chapter 10

1

Understanding Visual Communication Design

Digital design is not just about making things visually attractive on the screen. It encompasses research, planning, presentation, and programming. Before we jump into action, it is important to review the key ingredients that make visual communication design effective. The main focus is on understanding the content, who will be using it, and how design facilitates communication while empathizing with the users.

This chapter reviews the underlying framework in designing visual communication for the digital world. At the completion of this chapter, you will be able to:

- Describe the different types of content used in design projects.
- Define a user who will be interacting with the content.
- Communicate the content effectively using visual design principles.
- Explain the process of planning, designing, publishing, and managing a digital project.

Approaching a Digital Design Project

One of the most intimidating aspects for designers is determining how to begin a project. A common misstep is to immediately open a software package and start creating visuals. How can you successfully design a project when you know nothing about the project's subject matter? Designers must first read and understand the content they are trying to communicate.

Know the Context and Content

What is the difference between context and content? Context refers to a set of conditions or circumstances that are relevant to the situation. It answers who, what, when, where, how, and for what purpose; for example, the client's goals, resources, budget constraints, accessibility, and technology. Content refers to the actual intellectual message to be communicated.

No matter what digital device, the goal of screen design is to clearly and efficiently and effectively communicate content. You have probably heard the popular phrase, "Content is king!" The more you focus on the content, the easier the design decisions will be moving forward. So, what types of content do designers encounter?

- **Legacy content** already exists and needs to be edited, revised, and/or updated
- **Custom content** can be accessed from blogs and video posts
- **User-generated content** is user-controlled and may need to be moderated at a cost
- **Social media content** provides marketing opportunities but requires more maintenance to keep current
- **Legal content** are the client's privacy policies, copyright information, and terms and conditions

The connection between context, content, and users is fundamental to effective information architecture.

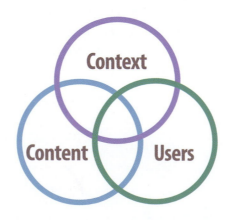

Define the Users

Linking the client's goals to the user's needs provides a specific objective toward which you can design. Whether you are designing for desktop, mobile, or wearable devices, you should focus on a "user-centered design." What does that mean? Design is about satisfying the user's needs and solving their problems. A user may be one individual or thousands; all with the same wants and needs. You are not the user and can't design something for everyone.

Defining the user goes beyond identifying common demographics such as age, gender, and location. Designers need to think about the entire user experience (often referred to as UX, UXD, or UED). Who will be using the project? Where will the project be viewed? When will the project be viewed? How will it be viewed? There are many distractions that can compete and/or interfere with your design. Defining the intended audience and how they will engage with the content provides a solid blueprint for success.

Designers have to understand the following about the intended users:

Audience: Age? Gender? Location? Income Levels? Education? Disabilities?

Environment: Home? Work? On-the-go? Noisy or quiet space? Outdoors or indoors?

Time: Leisure? Budgeted/time allotted? Quick check?

Device: Old? New? Bandwidth Issues? Connectivity Speeds?

Next, figure out what the users want. Why is the project being viewed? Users' motivation may come from a desire to learn more about something, curiosity, or it is required for their jobs. Just like clients, users have goals that will influence the final design. These goals and objectives include:

- **To Learn** – provide valuable and relevant information; repeat and reinforce the content; visualize data; break content into smaller modules for better retention; provide assessment tools such as tests to measure the user's progress

- **To Get Answers** – design searchable content and interaction; build navigation that promotes fast access to the content; avoid using long animation or time-consuming interactions

- **To Engage** – create a call-to-action button; provide clear and direct instructions; build in error prevention during the purchasing process; show user feedback and orientation; design elements that convey security in interacting with the project

- **To Explore** – add surprise and randomness to the interactions; create a navigational path that changes each time the project is used; provide multiple methods of navigation

Goals drive the design. Make sure the design solution satisfies the user's objectives and motivations.

Chapter 1 | Understanding Visual Communication Design

Finally, the project's design needs to empathize with the user. Users are emotional. They have needs, hopes, and fears. Designers affect users through visual communication. So, how do you learn from your users? In addition to describing the target audience, observe them in action. Users often make assumptions that will cause errors and disrupt the flow of the communication. Observation leads to a genuine understanding of how to solve a design problem and ultimately build a better project.

Empathy for the user includes discovering:

- What makes the users tick?
- What confuses them?
- What do they like and hate?
- Are there latent needs not yet addressed?

Don't lose sight of the user's feelings. Observe them in action.

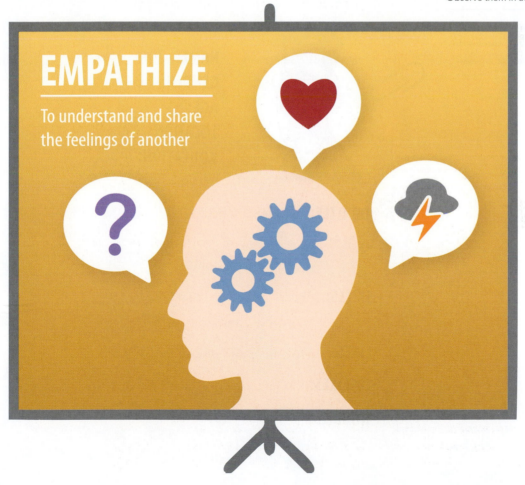

EMPATHIZE

To understand and share the feelings of another

In addition to observation, user information can also be collected through surveys, role playing, and interviews. The resulting data can be consolidated into a user persona. A persona is a fictional character that represents the "typical" user. It is a key concept in user-centered design. Personas capture the behavioral patterns, goals, skills, attitudes, and environment of different user types that will interact with your project.

Elements of a user persona include:

- Name and photo
- Demographics: age, gender, location, education
- Job title: role and responsibilities
- Goals: physical, social, and technological
- Skills: experience with technology and the subject matter
- Likes and dislikes

User personas represent the "typical" user. Data can come from observations including video recordings, surveys, and interviews.

NAME: Mike Johnson
GENDER: Male
AGE: 53
LOCATION: Ohio
EDUCATION: MBA

JOB TITLE: Business Analyst
GOALS: Be efficient at work, get promoted, simplify workload
SKILLS: Expert computer skills, speaks Spanish, very organized
LIKES: Travel, fast-paced activities
DISLIKES: Clutter, greasy foods, diet soda
HOBBIES: Photography, hiking

Outline the Project's Scope

Designers need to understand the intended scope of the project. From the initial client meetings, formulate how much work needs to be done and address where the final deliverable will reside and who will maintain it over time. If possible, identify any possible constraints and compensate for any delays. A well-planned project should provide clarity and a unified perspective on who is providing what to complete the project.

Include all required design components including a timeline that outlines milestone deliverables for the project over a period of time. Any additional client requests made outside of the approved plan are referred to as scope creep and can negatively impact the final design.

Ask the right questions to determine the project's scope.

Questions for the client:

- What is your goal in developing this project?
- Who are your users?
- Who are your competitors and do they have something similar?
- Who is providing the content?
- Is there a subject matter expert who can answer questions?
- Are there any existing logos or branding style guides to follow?
- Where will the final design reside?
- What tools does your company have to run, update, and manage the project?
- How long between project updates?
- Who will maintain the project over time?

Questions for the designer:

- Do I need to hire/collaborate with an expert?
  - ◊ Content strategist
  - ◊ Copy editor
  - ◊ Technology developer
  - ◊ Marketing strategist
- What additional expenses exist?
- Hardware and software?
- Server space?

Prioritize the Content

Once the content has been collected, it is essential to prioritize the information based on the defined goals and user needs. This is referred to as information architecture, making order out of chaos, which allows the user to find content and complete tasks without frustration. How you structure the content affects the user's response. Consider a hierarchical approach to present what the user needs to know.

Determine which content is primary and which can be secondary. Primary content addresses the users needs. Secondary content is supplemental. If the user does not access this content, it will not affect the user experience. The content is there if the user needs it. Use progressive disclosure of information to avoid overwhelming the user.

Designers should consider the following:

- Develop a visual content map
- Define the call-to-action needed when the user arrives at the home screen
- Develop page elements based on their purpose
- Determine the navigation to allow access to all high-priority content

Create a process and information flowchart. The process flowchart outlines the user's journey through the content. The information flowchart illustrates the information architecture.

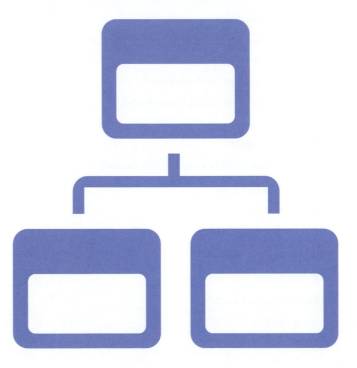

Chapter 1 | Understanding Visual Communication Design

Select the Right Tool for the Job

Designers need to carefully select the technology used to deliver a project to its intended audience. Don't blindly use the same tool for all design jobs. A tool that is right for one type of project does not mean it is right for everything. Designers sometimes get so lost in the technology and figuring out how to develop a project that they lose focus on the design objectives. Know what tools the client has to run, update, and manage the content in the future.

Designers need to understand the technology requirements and restrictions:

Online Tools:

- Adobe Dreamweaver, Muse, Edge Animate, HTML5 Boilerplates
- Restricts design control over certain interface elements and typography

Electronic Document Tools:

- Adobe InDesign and Acrobat Pro
- Limited interactivity and control of digital media

Presentation Tools:

- Adobe InDesign, Apple Keynote, Microsoft PowerPoint
- Limited interactivity beyond navigation and hyperlinks

Mobile App Tools:

- Apple XCode, Adobe InDesign
- Steep learning curve regarding programming interactions

Design Principles

Design is about communication. Designers need to apply proven design theories and methods. The visuals need to be aesthetically pleasing, promote consistency, and facilitate the user absorbing all the visual content on any given screen. Additionally, movement can clarify complex content or direct the user's eye. Finally, the experience needs to empathize with the user through affordances, mental and conceptual models, and existing user interface (UI) design patterns.

Visual Design Principles

Design principles are the building blocks used to create visual communication. They focus on the aesthetics by strategically implementing images, colors, fonts, and other elements. A successful visual design does not take away from the content on the page or function. Instead, it enhances the user experience by engaging the users and communicating content visually.

To review, when approaching a digital design project, first focus on the overall design as opposed to the individual elements. This is referred to as Gestalt. If the design elements are arranged properly, the Gestalt of the overall design will communicate more effectively. The key principles to incorporate include:

Alignment
- Creates order and a visual connection between elements on the screen.

Balance
- Symmetrical, or formal balance
- Eye seeks balance and symmetry
- Asymmetrical, or informal balance
- Adds more interest
- More abstract
- Overall composition still feels balanced even though there are differences in size, space, etc.

Contrast
- The juxtaposition of different elements used to create emphasis in a composition

Hierarchy
- The structuring of elements within a composition to visually show priority in the content

Proximity

- Creates relationships between elements to form a focal point
- How elements within a composition are grouped to appear as a single unit

Repetition

- Used to establish consistency and create a visual rhythm

Similarity

- Elements appear to be similar due to visual properties such as size, shape, and color

Space

- Includes the distance between, around, above, below, or within elements
- Both positive and negative spaces are important factors to be considered in every design

Unity

- How different elements within a composition interact with one another

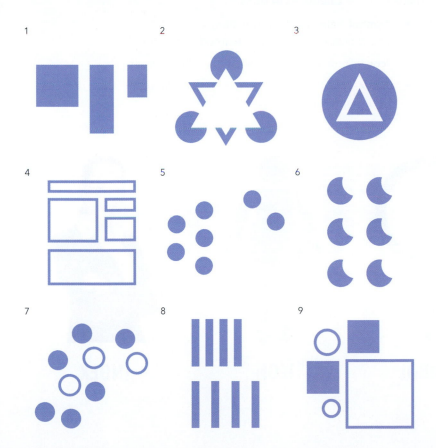

1
2
3
4
5
6
7
8
9

1 Alignment
2 Balance
3 Contrast
4 Hierarchy
5 Proximity
6 Repetition
7 Similarity
8 Space
9 Unity

Visual Semiotics and Design

Semiotics is the theory and study of signs (words and images) as elements of visual language for communication, and how they are interpreted. In visual semiotics, an object not only carries information and meaning, but also carries an emotional impact for the viewer.

When a sign is signaled to the audience through visual senses, the impression is sent to the brain, which leads to an interpretation of meaning – often subjective – depending on the perspective and experience of the viewer.

There are two kinds of meaning in semiotic theory:

- **Denotative** – literal meaning (what you see). An icon is denotative.
- **Connotative** – associated meaning (what you think). A symbol and index are connotative.

There are three **categories of signs**:

- **Symbol** – abstract representation, often arbitrary, of a concept that requires a learned connection.
- **Icon** – literal visual representation of the referent.
- **Index** – creates connection of concepts through visual representation.

SYMBOL   **ICON**   **INDEX**

Semiotic Model of Design

Every designed item has three distinct dimensions:

- **Semantic**
- **Syntactic**
- **Pragmatic**

Semantic – the relationship of meaning to the design. How well does the design represent the message? Do people fail to understand the message the design denotes? Does the design carry the same message in various cultures?

Syntactic – the relationship of formal aspects of the design to each other. How does the design look? How well do the parts of the design relate to each other? Is the construction of the design consistent in its use of visual principles?

Pragmatic – the relationship of a visual image to a user. Can a person use the design for its intended use? Is the design legible in typical viewing distances and lighting? Is the design difficult to reproduce?

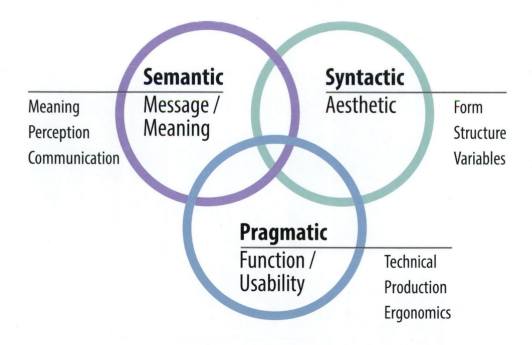

Motion Principles

The movement of images and text can be used to communicate complex ideas and concepts. Movement can also guide the user's eye and influence their interactions. For example, mobile devices are now implementing motion principles in the user interface to show transition from one screen to the next.

Motion can ease the user through the experience. It also assists with the visual hierarchy through how objects come on and off the screen, or into focus. The design challenge is using proper restraint when it comes to animating objects on the screen. Too much motion can sometimes be distracting or even confusing to the user. Motion should always be used to maintain or help focus on the content, not take it away.

Chapter 6 will cover these motion principles in detail:

- Anticipation
- Arcs
- Follow-through
- Overlapping actions
- Slow-in and slow-out
- Squash and stretch

1

2

3

4

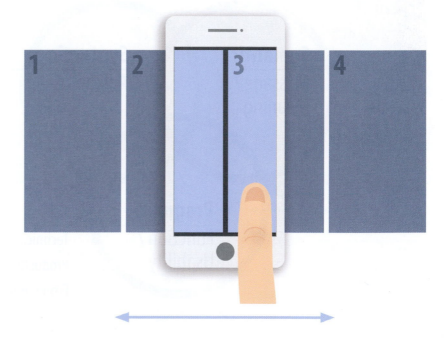

Examples of motion principles:

1 Anticipation
2 Slow-in and slow-out
3 Overlapping actions
4 Squash and stretch

User-Centered Design Process

Designers need to take a holistic approach to understanding the users, their tasks, and their environments. In order to achieve this, the users must be involved throughout the design and development process. This user-centered design process is iterative.

Successful user-centered design incorporates the following:

Affordances

- Visual clues that help users understand how to use an object

Mental and conceptual models

- Users predict how an object will behave based on previous experience
- Learned over time and built on top of one another

UI design patterns

- Using and repeating established design standards for:
  - ◊ the placement of graphical user interface assets
  - ◊ user interactions and feedback

User-centered design is a process that assists designers in creating interactive content and user interfaces that are learnable, usable, and fun.

The Digital Design Cycle

Designing for multiple screens and devices poses unique challenges. For example, the actual process of developing a website generally follows the same steps, from gathering the initial information, to the visual design and development, to the website's launch and maintenance. The process may vary slightly from designer to designer, but the basic cycle includes:

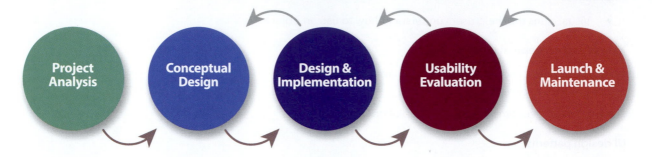

Analysis

- Identifying and defining the users and their needs
- Personas, profiles, accessibility
- Define the client's goals and objectives
- Planning the project goals and objectives to address the needs of the users
- Matrix of user tasks
- Workflow

Conceptual Design

- Gathering and organizing the information
- Information architecture and analysis of content
- Navigation plan
- User personas and scenarios
- Designing the visual look and feel
- Conceptual model
- Visual metaphors
- Design concepts
- Navigation design
- Storyboards and wireframes

Design and Implementation

- Designing the user interface
- Mockups
- Interaction flow
- Deference/clarity/depth
- Developing the underlying structure for the user's experience
- Layout: a collection of formats, styles, and grid systems
- Typography: a selection of typefaces and typesetting for the written content
- Color: to assist in communicating complex information or directing the user's eye
- Imagery: the use of visual semiotics, from photographically real to abstract icons and symbols
- Animation: a kinetic display of information using the element of time
- Interaction: moving from passive to active user involvement
- Sequencing: visual storytelling techniques to break the content up into manageable "chunks"
- Sound: the use of abstract, vocal, or music

Usability Evaluation

- Testing the effectiveness of the experience throughout each stage
- Making iterative improvements based on the evaluation results

Launch and Maintenance

- Delivering the site to device(s)
- Maintaining the site to keep it current

Summary

This chapter reviewed the underlying framework for designing visual communication for the digital world. Designers need to apply proven design theories and methods. They need to take a holistic approach to understanding the users, their tasks, and their environments. The visuals need to be aesthetically pleasing, promote consistency, and facilitate the user absorbing all the content on any given screen.

Digital design encompasses research, planning, presentation, and programming. You should now be able to:

- Describe the different types of content used in design projects.
- Define a user who will be interacting with the content.
- Communicate the content effectively using visual design principles.
- Explain the process of planning, designing, publishing, and managing a digital project.

The next chapter focuses on presentation design.

2

Creating a Visual Presentation

Visual presentations ... we have all sat through these at some point, and many of us have presented. But what makes a good visual presentation? Information hierarchy, visual organization, manageable content, and approaching the presentation as a narrative can help achieve the goal.

In this chapter we will explore the principles and techniques that will help you create informative, successful visual presentations. Upon the completion of this chapter, you will be able to:

- Outline key concepts and ideas to create a narrative flow.
- Integrate visual design principles into effective presentation layout to engage the audience.
- Use brevity to deliver the message.
- Integrate information design principles.

Presentation Design

The design of visual presentations goes beyond just selection of software and putting together some type and images to project on a screen. It is a form of information design. Communication of a specific message with visual presentations requires understanding the intent of the presentation and the intended audience, as well as visual design principles.

The visual presentation should support the speaker's message. It is not a document to be read. The audience should be able to balance listening to the speaker and reading brief information on the screen that reinforces what is being said. On average, most people will only remember three items at a time, so make sure they are the critical items. If you have too much information on-screen, the audience will lose focus on the speaker.

Outlining key concepts and ideas that are being presented will help in narrowing down the amount of information on each slide. Simplicity and brevity are an essential. Complex information needs to be made clear to the audience. Presentations can leave a lasting impression. Make it a good one.

Key visual design principles, information design methodology, and technical issues must be considered and integrated.

- Design process
- Visual organization systems: grids, template development, structure and sequence, proportion, placement, color palette
- Typography
- Information hierarchy
- Visual components: images, diagrams, charts, video, color
- Audience: culture, language, age
- Terminology: use of effective verbs, keywords, headings and titles
- Designing your own effective layout templates for presentations
- Limitations of projection
- Distance
- Pace
- Media integration

Five main elements of good presentation design:

1 The message is the focus
2 Keep the presentation simple
3 Use readable fonts and limit text quantity
4 Use impactful images that strengthen the message
5 Use colors that complement the overall theme

Developing the Presentation

Questions to ask when developing a presentation:

- What is the topic and content?
- Who is delivering it?
- What is the purpose of the event?
- Who is the audience?
- What is the physical location – type of room?
- How is it being presented – technical equipment; is it on large projection screens, computers monitors, laptops, tablets?

Designing the Narrative Flow

Have a clear outline of the content and create a **narrative flow.** The presenter is telling a story as the content unfolds through each slide. The audience has to quickly scan and process what they see/read on the slide and turn their attention back to the presenter. Remember, slides are for the audience, not the presenter. Slides help to deliver key information, ideas, and emotions.

The purpose of a narrative flow is to allow for focus, sequence, organization, and connections within the information being presented to the audience. Keep these key points in mind:

- Divide the information into "**chunks,**" much like chapters in a book.
- Identify **key points** that need to be highlighted for the audience.
- Provide no more than 3 key points on the slide at one time. Additional slides can always be used.
- Keep the text brief and focused.

Books on presentation design:

Slideology: The Art and Science of Creating Great Presentations
by Nancy Duarte

Presentation Zen: Simple Ideas on Presentation Design and Delivery
by Garr Reynolds

Stories that Move Mountains: Storytelling and Visual Design for Persuasive Presentations
by Martin Sykes, A. Nicklas Malik, and Mark D. West

SLIDESHOW

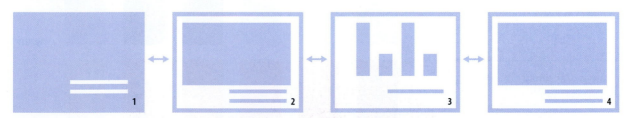

Presentation Design Components

Information Architecture

Establishing a hierarchy of the overall structure and organization of the content is a key component of presentation design. The design process is part of that architecture. The following describes steps and components of visual presentation design.

- **Identify the audience**: Who will see this presentation?
- **Outline the content:** Create an outline of the content to be presented.
- **Look for inspiration** in the content to help you with the visual design.

Ideation and Theme

Sketch concepts for the layout. A visual theme should relate to the presentation content. Avoid using prebuilt themes, like those found in some of the templates in the software being used. There also needs to be consistency in the design to create a unified presentation. Create a captivating opening title slide. It should be related yet distinct from content slides.

Color

Color can be subtle, and yet powerful. Pick a **color scheme** that represents the theme. Color meaning also varies from culture to culture and a designer needs to be sensitive to the audience when conveying a theme. Color can also be used to highlight text such as hyperlinks, web page links, and keywords.

There are tools to help you in developing color themes. Maria Claudia Cortes' *Color in Motion* is an interactive site that explains colors and their meaning in various cultures.
color.adobe.com
colourlovers.com
mariaclaudiacortes.com

This example is the color palette used for this book.

Typography

Readability is the most important aspect of the type choice. Not all typefaces work well for presentations. There are some typefaces that lend themselves to effective screen use. The audience has to review any presented text quickly and turn their attention back to the presenter.

Think about the message you are conveying and complement it with appropriate typography choices. Typefaces can also set a mood to complement the overall visual theme. **Typographic hierarchy** must also be considered. Size and weight are helpful in achieving this. Use only one or two typefaces within the presentation. Color and style can create emphasis without adding more typefaces.

Berthold Akzidenz Grotesk

Helvetica Neue

Georgia

Bookman

Didot

Comic Sans

Brush Script

Papyrus

Some typefaces have better legibility on screen and for projection than others. Serif fonts work well for large text elements, but readability declines for smaller type sizes.

Sans serif fonts are more effective for presentation design. Of course, good typography is dependent on the spacing, size, placement, and kerning of the font.

For more information on using grid systems:

thegridsystem.com

The Grid
by Kim Elam

Making and Breaking the Grid
by Timothy Samara

Grid Structure

A grid is the most basic, yet integral part of visual organization systems. The grid structure will help keep consistency, unity, and hierarchy intact throughout the presentation layout. It is the most effective way to organize content.

Modular Grid

Column Grid

Hierarchical Grid

Master Template

The master template should contain any elements and information that repeat on consecutive slides, such as title, event name, consecutive numbering, or background color. Do not overfill the master template as visual clutter will deteriorate the communication of the presentation. There is usually a main master template for the main title slide; a secondary master template for divider slides for managing content into sections; and a template for the body of the slides.

Visual Clutter

Keep the presentation simple and not cluttered or full of visual fluff. Focus on the meaningful. Keep text to a minimum. Highlight important aspects. Leave the rest for the verbal portion of the presentation by the presenter. When using a background image, make sure it does not visually compete with the elements placed on top of it (type, images, data, charts, graphic elements).

Slide is visually cluttered. Too many pictures for the message to be clear.

Title too busy with this style of shadow and all capital letters are harder to read quickly

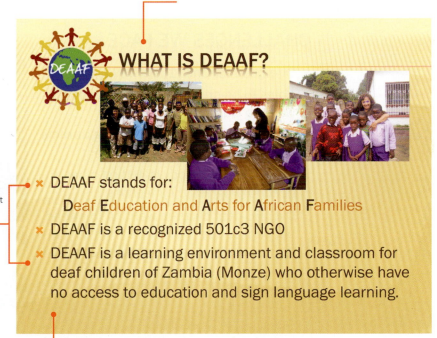

Too much text to read, line space too tight, and colored type and bullets are not readable against background

Background too busy and deters audience from message

Visual Hierarchy

All content is not equal. There has to be a relationship between elements. Slides that are not cluttered allow for focus by the audience on the main information being conveyed. By using size, placement, proximity, direction, and contrast, you can build the hierarchy of the visual elements on the slides. This will help direct the audience in processing what they see/read. It is better to add additional slides for content, rather than cramming one with too much information.

Bullet point fatigue:

Overuse of bullet points makes it hard to focus on what is really important. There are other creative ways to highlight information without just using bullet points. Break up content onto more than one slide. The presenter will discuss details so the audience should not have to read everything on the screen.

Title too busy with shadow and all capital letters are harder to read quickly

CHALLENGES WE FACE

- Dire need for One (1) or Two (2) Bore
- Holes to be drilled to provide fresh water to classroom
- Lack of a secure school building attracts child rapists and criminal element
- Current student body is getting older and need to progress their lessons
- Over 60 deaf children wanting to attend but cannot due to distance from school – Dorms would ease the struggle of daily commute on foot for 4+ miles radius.

Too many bullet items for one slide

Too much text to read within each bullet statement

Relationship between elements:

Order, size, placement, and contrast can help in building the visual organization of the content.

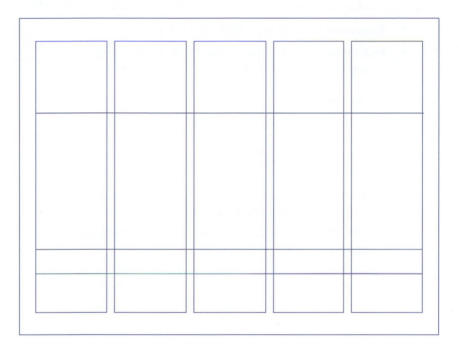

- **Deaf Education & Arts for African Families**
- **501(c)3 NGO**
- **Learning environment for Deaf children in Monze, Zambia**

What is DEAAF?

Imagery

Images can create a stronger impact than just words on a screen. They are more memorable. Imagery can be divided into two main categories for a presentation:

- **Supportive:** Topic photos, symbols, backgrounds.
- **Explanatory:** Visual shapes, icons, charts, graphs, diagrams, tables, and maps.

Supportive Imagery

Original
- Background overwhelms content
- Too many bullet points for one slide
- Text is tight and overfills the slide
- No visual support for the content

Revised
- Highlight key points on individual slides
- Presenter can verbally explain details
- Imagery supports key information being presented

Use quality imagery. When using photographic images that have been improperly stretched or pixelated, it looks unprofessional and your audience will notice. Only use images that are your own, purchased, or appropriately free. Do not use anything for which you do not have permission. Check the licensing. Give credit to the creator of the image when appropriate. Use images that will scale properly. Size photos at 1024 x 768 (or other if designing for a specific device) so that you can reduce images if needed.

Explanatory Imagery

Image resolution ranges from 72 ppi to 300 ppi, with 150 ppi as an acceptable mid-range for most screen presentations.

Original

- Background overwhelms content
- Too many bullet points for one slide
- No visual support for the content

Revised

- Simplified to express the main content
- Presenter can verbally explain details
- Imagery supports key information being presented
- Color continuity system

Websites about information design:

informationdesign.org

iiid.net

infosthetics.com

Maps
- Continent shown in full, with individual country indicated through color change
- Detailed country map shows cities
- Allows for the audience to have a better comprehension of the geography and physical locations.

Information Design

Information design is the process and application of making information understandable, accessible, and visually engaging to the user. With the diversity of audiences, **information has to be communicated effectively**, not just attractively. Remember that content is king. Information design is a visual explanation of content. Don't just make pretty talking points. Instead, display information in a way that makes complex information clear.

Some key elements of effective information design:

- Visual organization of content
- Representation of ideas in visual form
- Clarity of processes and quantitative information
- Transmission of information to increase efficiency of understanding and comprehension
- Color is functional, not just decorative
- Solutions can be two-dimensional or three-dimensional
- Quantitative content should be "true" and not altered for the sake of design

Applications of information design include diagrams, maps, charts, tables, icons, documents, and wayfinding.

Media Integration

Motion, sound, video, hyperlinks, and interactivity can be integrated into a visual presentation. With Adobe InDesign you can:

- Make anything into a button or link
- Create interactive links to external files
- Place video and audio within InDesign
- Export as an interactive PDF

Software

There is a variety of software on the market for presentation development. You can create a presentation and then export as a PDF. Multi-page/multi-slide software works best for creating effective presentations, such as:

- **Adobe InDesign**
- **Apple Keynote**
- **Microsoft PowerPoint**

While many designers do not like using PowerPoint or Keynote, you may have a client that uses it and needs to make updates and changes to the files. You must be able to develop the presentations in software that meets their needs. Some businesses do not use Adobe InDesign or similar products for their office work. Microsoft Office is often the in-house software. Not every business has a designer on staff, and they might not be able to hire one every time they make edits or upgrade their presentations.

Books that provide an overview of information design:

The Information Design Handbook
by Jenn Visocky O'Grady
and Ken Visocky

The Wall Street Journal Guide to Information Graphics: The Dos and Don'ts of Presenting Data, Facts, and Figures
by Dona M. Wong

Technical Settings

Aspect ratio is the ratio of the width of the screen to the height of the screen.

Presentation Sizes

- Use standard sizes for presentations
  - ◊ Commonly used in the past has been 1024 x 768 (4:3 ratio)
  - ◊ Many projection units now use an aspect ratio of 1280 x 720 (16:9 ratio).
- Some situations will require a different setting. If you know what types of projection/viewing devices will be used, plan your presentation accordingly.

Standard presentation screen sizes.

4:3 ratio

16:9 ratio (cinematic aspect ratio)

There are thousands of screen widths available and you cannot design for every one of them.

For example:

- **320 px:** Smartphone Portrait
- **480 px:** Smartphone Landscape
- **768 px:** Tablet Portrait
- **960 px:** Tablet Landscape
- **1024 px:** Large Tablet
- **1280 px:** Laptop
- **1440 px:** Widescreen Desktop

1024 x 768

1280 x 720

Color Settings

- Use RGB for screen presentations.

Image Resolution

- 72 to 300 ppi are fine. 150 ppi is an acceptable mid-range resolution.
- The image should be the actual size or slightly larger than the size to be used in the presentation.

Image File Type

- JPEG is commonly used for image files.
- PNG and BMP are often used for screen and web pages (low resolution).
- TIFF can be used for transparent imagery such as a logo (if you do not want a solid color block).
- EPS is best for line art or vector graphics.

For more information on color basics:
www.usability.gov/how-to-and-tools/
methods/color-basics.html

RGB

Color system for screens

consists of:

- Red
- Green
- Blue

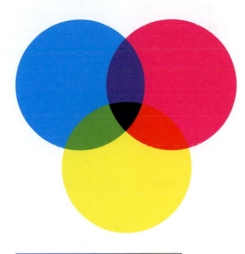

CMYK

Ink color system for printing

consists of:

- Cyan
- Magenta
- Yellow
- Black

Chapter Case Study:
Designing a PDF Presentation
for a Non-Profit Organization

This case study uses **Adobe InDesign** for creating a PDF presentation. InDesign allows you to create interactive presentations through its tools, as well as export to a PDF. The master page functions, grid structure control, style panels, and ability to integrate interactivity, motion, video, and sound make it a desirable tool.

Master Pages, Grids, and Duplication are used to make it easy to organize repetitive items and be consistent with the design.

Part 1: Collecting Content

Images, text, logos, and other media (video, sound if applicable) should be collected and organized. Be aware of any requirements regarding company identity guidelines. For this presentation, the logo, images, and text were provided by DEAAF founder and president, Lisa Zahra.

Part 2: Planning

A discussion between client and designer should take place before beginning the visual development. Examples of questions to ask:

- What is the main objective of the presentation?
- What key points need to be made?
- Who is the audience?
- How will it be shown (computer, projection, room size, etc.)?
- How much time will be allotted to present?

An **outline** is helpful in developing a presentation. Setting up the flow of the content will make it easier to develop the slides.

Gather information to develop the presentation.

Client: DEAAF

Presenter: Lisa Zahra

Audience: Social/Community clubs and organizations, schools, and churches.

Purpose: To inform the audience about DEAAF and encourage support and donations.

Venues: Classrooms, meeting rooms, church halls.

Equipment: Laptop provided by presenter. Projection or monitor displays will vary based on location.

Time Allotted: Presenter is limited to approximately 20 minutes.

Part 3: Document Setup

A new document was opened with InDesign. The setup is **1024 x 768 pixels**. This is a standard size. The intent can be **Web** or **Digital Publishing**. Either can be used for designing a presentation. Primary Text Frame must be **de-selected** as you do not need that for slides.

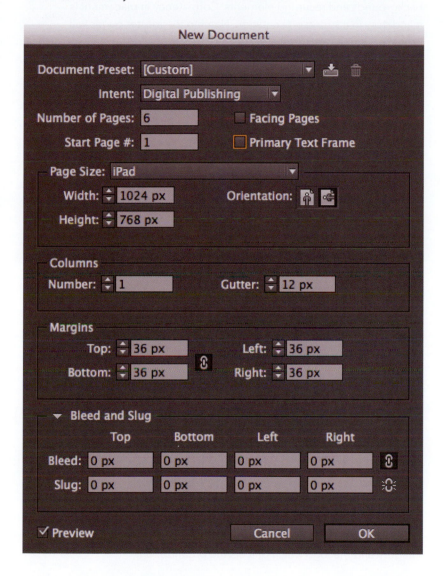

The margins and columns can be changed once the document is created.

These layers were created: **Text, Images,** and **Back**. Any image needed as a background but not on the master page was placed on the **Back layer.**

Recurring elements – background images and logo were placed on **Master pages.** Multiple master pages make it easier to manage backgrounds and recurring elements. Consistency in placement is mandatory in a strong presentation. Naming the master pages will help you keep it organized.

A **grid** is setup on the **Master Page A** using **Layout > Margins and Columns.** Then the master page is duplicated three times and named **B–Landscape, C–Water, D–Money.** Background images were added to each master page. The DEAAF logo was then added to each of these pages.

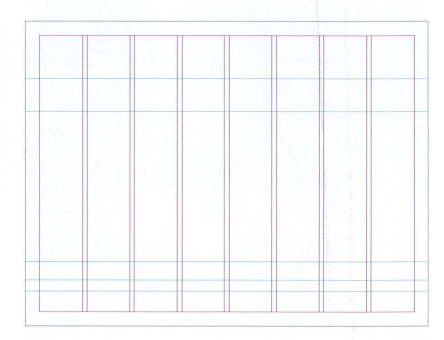

Part 4: Color

Colors used for the presentation are based on colors in the photographic imagery and the logo which reflects the organization.

Part 5: Content and Visual Communication

The **title slide** should **make an impact** to gain the attention of the audience. DEAAF president Lisa Zahra and other board members present to various groups in two countries, including Rotary Clubs International, Deaf advocates, businesses, high school and college student clubs, church groups, individuals, and volunteer organizations.

The title slide uses the DEAAF logo as part of design layout. So it is not added on the A-Master page.

Each subsequent slide is basically set up the same, but with changing textual content and images. The grid is used consistently. The background images relate to the content on the individual slides. The logo is present, but does not dominate the slide.

Remember: The presenter will verbalize information. It does not need to be on screen. Do not overload the slide with text. The audience should not be trying to read large quantities of text while the presenter is speaking and making their points.

Part 5: Typography

A **sans-serif** typeface was used for the text in the presentation. It is best to work with one to two typefaces. Sans serif was preferred by both the client and designer for the DEAAF presentation. To use a serif typeface could become too busy with the imagery being used. Some of the audience members are deaf and have to read the screen because of their hearing limitations. In that case, a script could be provided, or an interpreter is on hand, or captioning is incorporated. Lisa is a certified sign-language interpreter, so she is able to interpret while presenting.

The typeface chosen, its size, and color along with the quantity of typographic content relates to several factors that can affect audience comprehension:

- Language differences
- Vision quality
- Lightness or darkness of room
- Size of projection or screen

The typography can help to set a mood in addition to presenting content.

Clean typography, simple graphics, and photographic images relating to the subject can create an effective presentation.

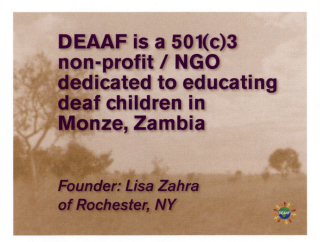

Part 6: Slide Transition

As shown in the slides below, additional text is added after the slide is duplicated. This is done to allow for transitions to be added to the slides. You can add page transitions within InDesign, as well as buttons and hyperlinks. If so, then you must **Export** the InDesign file as an **Interactive PDF** so the interaction will be embedded. You can also add additional interactivity in **Adobe Acrobat.**

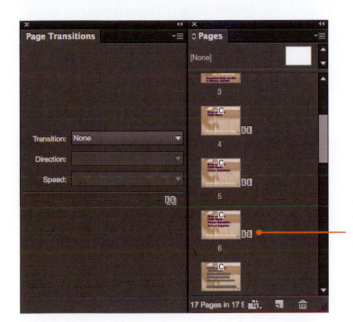

This icon appears once a transition is applied to the page.

The presentation follows these guidelines:

- Simplified to express the main content
- Presenter can verbally explain details
- Imagery supports key information being presented
- Color continuity system

- Bore Hole for fresh water
- Power Generator
- School Supplies

Immediate Needs

- Bore Hole for fresh water
- Power Generator
- School Supplies
- Monetary Donations

Immediate Needs

- Classroom Building

Long-term Needs

- Classroom Building
- Electricity

Long-term Needs

- Classroom Building
- Electricity
- Dormitory

Long-term Needs

- Classroom Building
- Electricity
- Dormitory
- Security Fence

Long-term Needs

The use of a slight drop shadow on the text helps to make it visually **pop** from the background.

When using **graphs** or other information graphics, keep it simple. Notice there are no extra lines that you typically see on graphs. This keeps the **focus on the content.**

Colorful images are on a neutral background to avoid visual conflict. Limiting the number of images at one time also helps in audience attention and comprehension.

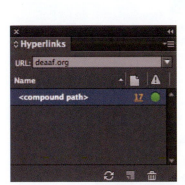

Sometimes the presenter has a video to show. This can be added within InDesign using the menu **Window > Interactive > Media.**

A **hyperlink** was added to the last slide for the website. The text **DEAAF.org** was converted with **Type > Create Outlines**. Then open **Window > Interactive > Hyperlinks**. The object text is selected and then type or paste the web **URL.** Once this is completed, there will be a dotted line box around the object indicating there is a link in your file. The dotted line will not be visible in the interactive PDF. The cursor will change when rolling over the link in the PDF indicating it is a link.

Part 7: Exporting the Presentation File

While creating the presentations, it was saved as an InDesign file.
Always save a version in this format so that it can be adjusted as needed.

Once completed, the file was **Exported** as a **PDF (Interactive).** It was saved
with the settings shown. Choices for resolution and image quality allow
you to save the PDF based on the presentation situation (projection, room
size, device, and such).

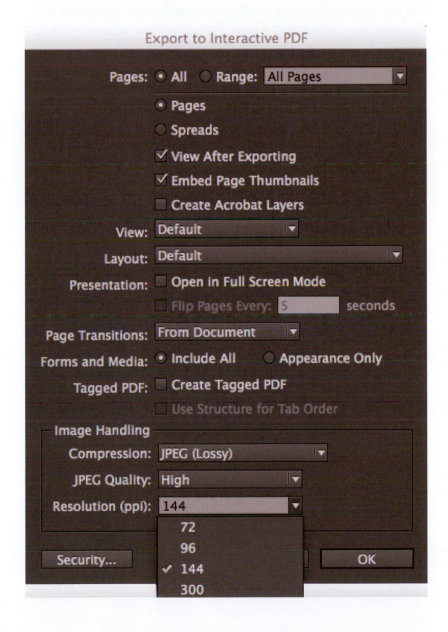

Summary

A visual presentation needs to support the speaker's message. It is not a document to be read. The audience should be able to balance listening to the speaker and viewing brief information to read on the screen that supports what is spoken. Information hierarchy, visual organization, manageable content, and approaching the presentation as a narrative can help achieve the goal.

You can apply the principles and processes presented in this chapter to designing visual presentations, regardless of the actual software used.

This completes the chapter; you should now be able to:

- Outline key concepts and ideas to create a narrative flow.
- Integrate visual design principles into an effective presentation layout to engage the audience.
- Use brevity to deliver the message on screen.
- Integrate information design principles.
- Manage media and interactivity integration.

The next chapter will focus on user interface design.

3

Prototyping a User Interface (UI) Design

Visual designers are an integral part of a team developing an application. Designing a successful interface requires understanding visual design and interaction principles as related to the user. UI is a form of communication with the user. From sketch to prototype, a combination of technical workflow, user testing, and design principles are integrated. Knowing your user, the content, and method of digital delivery and devices will aid in creating effective user interface prototypes.

This chapter reviews the process for designing effective user interfaces. Upon the completion of this chapter, you will be able to:

- Integrate design thinking, ideation, and sketching.
- Apply visual design principles to an interactive interface design.
- Understand the process of designing an effective user interface through prototyping.

The designer needs to be aware of UI guidelines for the various digital platforms. Here are some helpful links:

developer.apple.com

msdn.microsoft.com/

developer.samsung.com/

What Is Prototype Design?

Organization is key in planning an effective user interface. As discussed in Chapter 1, how can you successfully design a project when you know nothing about the project's subject matter? Designers must first read and understand the content they are trying to communicate. Then you will need to identify and analyze your audience/user. You must also comprehend what the final product will be in order to plan and design an effective user interface. The overall user experience (**UX**) is directly impacted by the user interface design (**UI**).

The key to effective prototyping of a user interface is understanding your audience. Knowing who they are and how they relate to the content can make or break the interface effectiveness.

A prototype is not a wireframe, but a mid- to high-fidelity representation of the final product. It should simulate interaction to allow the user to interface with the function and content. The prototype should allow for testing interactions similar to the final version of the product.

UI / User Interface Design	UX / User Experience Design
• Look and Feel	• Strategy and Content
• Responsiveness and Interactivity	• Wireframing and Prototyping
	• Execution and Analytics

UI Design

Tapping into the emotional experience can help to make a strong imprint on the user. You want the user to feel a sense of humanity, not like a machine. They need to make a connection with the interaction.

There are 3 types of design that relate to UI design:

- **Emotional Design**
- **Persuasive Design**
- **Service Design**

Important considerations for a user interface:

- **Work with the real users:** Work with the people that will use the application. Having them evaluate throughout the process can create a much stronger and effective solution.

- **Accessibility and usability:** Issues that the design must address for users with disabilities.

- **Impression or Appeal:** The initial visual and organizational appearance of the UI makes an impact on the user, often subconsciously. Familiarity and metaphor can also create a positive appeal for the user.

- **Behavior:** The UI helps the user interact and understand the content. The design should not compete with it. Users have set ways of interacting through experience. Draw upon that experience to make the interface familiar and easy to use. Visual feedback and consistent navigation are vital to a successful UI.

- **Keep it simple:** Avoid clutter. Don't make the UI difficult. Ease of use is key to effective UI solutions. The user needs to have a pleasurable experience, not a negative one. Fulfill the needs of the user.

- **Hierarchy, Pattern, and Consistency:** A sense of structure, order, and sequence allow the user to stay focused and accomplish tasks. The visual elements (color, type, space, images) are integrated into the UI to make it more effective for the user.

- **Prototype actuality:** Do not prototype functions that you cannot possibly deliver. Stick to what you can actually provide.

For more information about UI design, read:

About Face: The Essentials of Interaction Design by Alan Cooper and Robert Reimann

The Elements of the User Experience by Jesse James Garrett

Interactive Design: An introduction to the Theory and Application of User-centered Design by Andy Pratt

Gestalt Principles of Perception and UI

The visual principles of Gestalt are the fundamental rules of human psychology in terms of visual perception and have a direct relationship to human-computer interaction design. These are especially relevant in designing the user interface. (Refer to Chapter 1 for more information on design principles).

1. **Proximity** – the law of proximity states that when we perceive a collection of objects, we will see objects close to each other as forming a group.

2. **Similarity** – the law of similarity states that elements will be grouped perceptually if they are similar to each other (size, shape, color, etc.).

3. **Prägnanz** (figure-ground) – the law of Prägnanz (figure-ground) states the idea that in perceiving a visual field, some objects take a prominent role (the figures) while others recede into the background (the ground).

4. **Symmetry** – the law of symmetry states that when we perceive objects we tend to perceive them as symmetrical shapes that form around their center.

5. **Closure** – the law of closure states that we perceptually close, or complete, objects that are not, in fact, complete.

6. **Hierarchy** – the law of hierarchy is the order in which the human eye perceives what it sees.

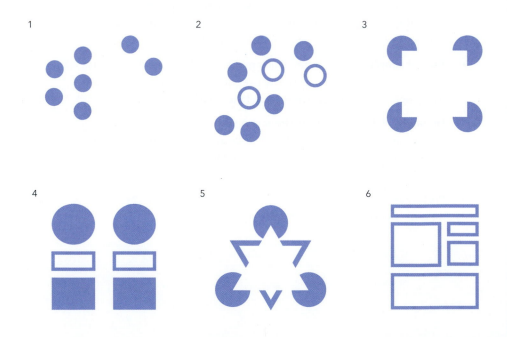

Considerations for Functionality

The interaction establishes the rules for how the user engages with the content. Chapter 4 covers interaction design in more detail. Here is an overview of user interface guidelines to consider when developing the interface and interaction:

- Aesthetic Integrity
- Visual Metaphors
- Perception and Manipulation
- Consistency
- User Control
- Affordance
- Predictability
- Efficiency
- Responsiveness/Feedback
- Explorability
- Forgiveness

For more information about information architecture, visit these sites:

com/information_architecture_30

webstyleguide.com/wsg3/3-information-architecture/index.html

boxesandarrows.com/integrating-prototyping-into-your-design-process/

Icons can be used for navigation. Three main categories are:

Abstract – indirect meaning

Metaphorical – represents function

Pictorial – depiction of object and its function

For more information on usability principles, read *Visual Usability: Principles and Practices for Designing Digital Applications* by Tania Schlatter and Deborah Levin

Visual Design Components

Typefaces, images, color, graphic elements, icons, and branding elements have to work in a cohesive design for the site, and support the **hierarchy of information** being presented to the user.

Visual considerations when designing the site prototype:

Typography

- Use a limited number of typefaces
- Size, weight, color, style of the typeface

Graphic elements

- Rules and bars
- Icons and symbols

Branding requirements (should follow company guidelines)

- Color system
- Typeface
- Identity mark
- Photographic style
- Imagery
- Photographs
- Illustrations

Navigation

- Call-to-action
- Buttons
- Symbols
- Actions
- Breadcrumbs

The Design Process Refined

While there is an overall project process, with prototyping you need to focus on the user experience and testing before final refinement and implementation. Designing a prototype allows for testing and revision without going into full-blown production. You don't want to spend hours – and dollars – formally designing and programming an interface without testing the concept and usability.

Process Steps

Steps that will help you in developing your prototypes for interactive projects:

- Research
- Planning
- Content requirements
- Design ideation and brainstorming
- Information architecture
- Sketching concepts
- Wireframes
- Evaluation and testing iteration
- Mockups
- Evaluation and testing iteration
- Prototyping
- Evaluation and testing iteration
- Development

For further reading about user interface (UI) design, read:

UI is Communication: How to Design Intuitive, User Centered Interfaces by Focusing on Effective Communication by Everett N McKay

Digital Design Essentials: 100 Ways to Design Better Desktop, Web, and Mobile Interfaces by Rajesh Lal

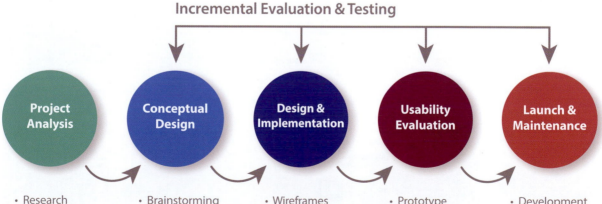

Incremental Evaluation & Testing

Project Analysis	Conceptual Design	Design & Implementation	Usability Evaluation	Launch & Maintenance
• Research • Planning • Content requirements	• Brainstorming • Information architecture • Sketching concepts	• Wireframes *(low-fidelity)* • Mockups *(mid-fidelity)*	• Prototype *(high-fidelity)*	• Development • Implementation

Planning

The designer needs to organize and plan for the layout of the interface. Developing a written outline of the content structure, building the site map, and identifying related functionality will help organize the prototype design.

Information architecture determines the necessary content, its priority, and where and when it will appear in the final project.

Preliminary sketches and organizational charting help with visualizing the actions and order of the design. Another method often used is sticky notes. The ability to move these around can help in the planning stage of design. This also allows for group interaction. Both of these are informal methods meant for ideation and development of the organization, interaction, and navigation of the project that lead to prototypes.

Developing the "look and feel" of the design (i.e., metaphor, style, theme, branding considerations) will happen after the initial organization, function identification, and wireframe development.

Brainstorming sketches for an interactive app design. Image: courtesy of Kaige Liu

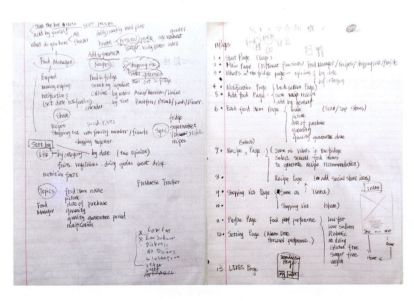
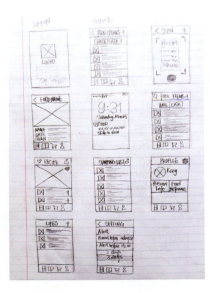

Information Architecture

The site map and content need to have a clear hierarchy the user can easily perceive. Organizing both the overall content, and then the page content, will help to maintain an effective interface. Information architecture is the structural design for the navigation of information to allow for intuitive access to content.

- **Flowchart**: Shows the sequence of steps to accomplish a task within the interface and to identify the usability steps.

- **Site Map Hierarchy**: Organizes the flow and structure of the content of the digital application or web page. The site map provides a high-level overview of the site or app.

- **Content Hierarchy**: Grids and box models help to visually identify the theme and organize the hierarchy of content on the page-view level.

To learn more about information architecture, read *Information Architecture for the World Wide Web: Designing for the Web and Beyond* by Louis Rosenfeld and Peter Morville.

Example of a site map for a non-profit organization.

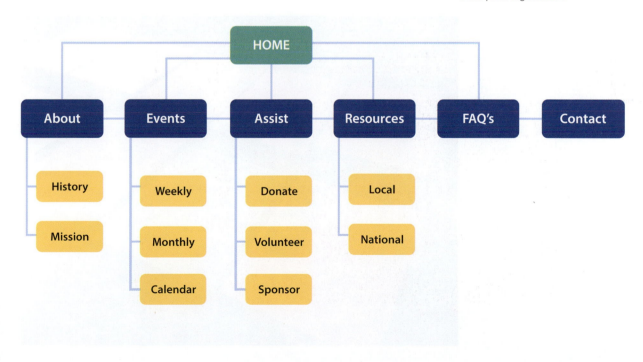

Sketching Concepts

Manual drawings and sticky notes work well for initial concept development. Both allow for **quick ideation** and change. Once you have a concept and want to refine it further, software comes into play to build a box model.

For more information about developing concepts, read *Sketching User Experiences: The Workbook* by Saul Greenberg and Sheelagh Carpendale.

Ideation sketches for an interactive app design.

Top Image: courtesy of Kaige Liu

Bottom Image: courtesy of Tejal Sampat.

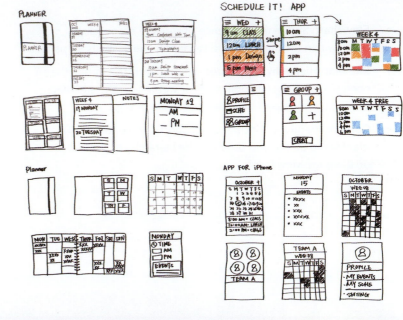

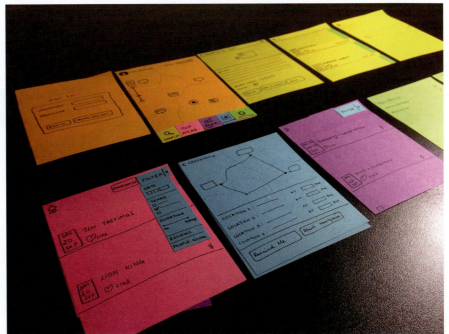

Chapter 3 | Prototyping a User Interface Design

Wireframing

Now that you have the content and users identified, organized the content, and have sketched some concepts, you are ready to build a visual **wireframe**. It does not need to define any particular style and you don't have to identify typefaces or main colors at this point. Just focus on the initial layout concept to show information organization.

In addition to manual sketches, there is a variety of software and apps for this step, but it should relate to the final delivery device. Depending on the output, using a combination of an app and software may be more effective for the prototype stage (for a partial list, refer to "ideation tools" later in this chapter).

Grid

One of the main components of an effective interface design is the **underlying grid.** This serves as a consistent organizational element. Using a grid will keep the design looking consistent from screen to screen. The grid should be developed after the initial concept, and be incorporated into your box model. Be sure to make it adaptable to media requirements as you develop your prototype.

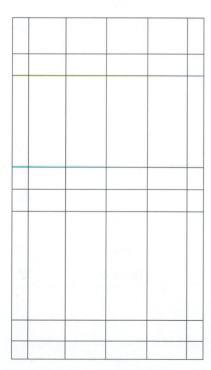
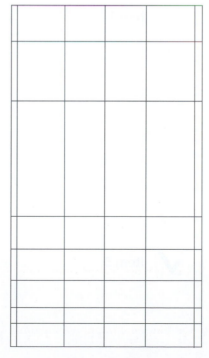

Two examples of grids used for app designs.

Wireframe Elements

When creating wireframes, use simple graphics to represent **interaction components**. Be sure to allow enough space for the user's finger to interact when tapping a touch device. The average height needed is 50px.

1 Text field
2 Button
3 Hamburger button
4 Radio button
5 Check box
6 Drop-down list
7 List box
8 Combo box

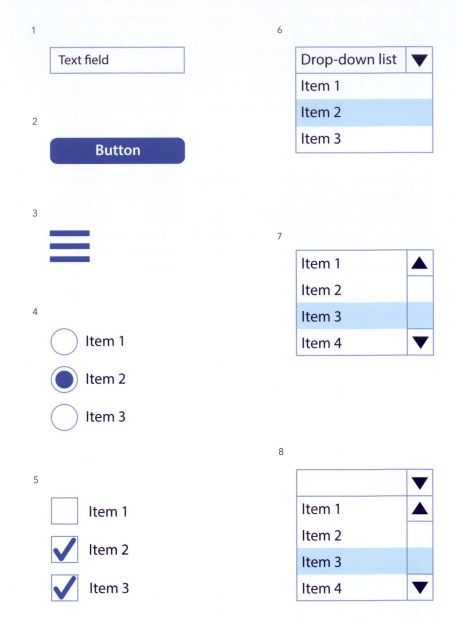

Menu Navigation Structures

There are several common structures for **navigation menus**:

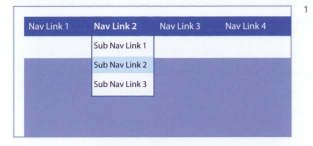

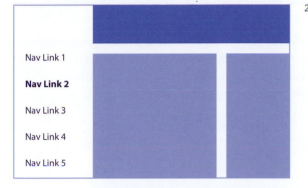

1 Drop-down
2 Persistent
3 Slider
4 Tabs

Box Model Wireframe

The **box model wireframe** method allows for visual organization of elements, typographic hierarchy, navigation location, and content placement. It also allows for easy movement of the elements to try various arrangements. At this stage, there are no set images, colors, or typefaces.

A **wireframe** is a **low-fidelity** representation of a design. This is a basic rough stage that is usually black and white and should clearly show

- the main groups of content
- the structure of information
- description/basic visualization of the user interface interaction

The wireframe is the base of your design and should have representation of every element of the final product. Once the initial concept is approved, the site visual layout can be fleshed out and incorporate color, typographic style, and imagery in the level of design.

Low-fidelity box model sketches of an app, *Roc Doc,* by Yue Liu.

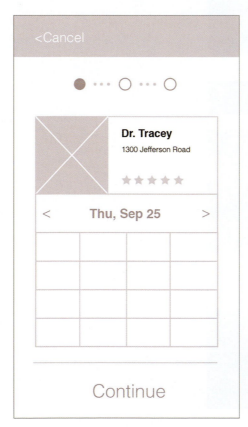
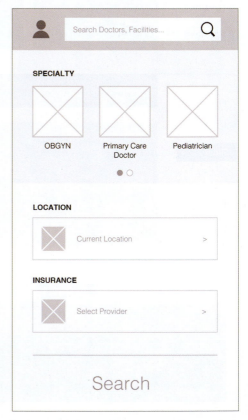

Mockup

The **mockup** stage of the process is considered a **mid-** to **high-fidelity** design representation. A mockup should

- represent the information structure
- visualize the content
- demonstrate basic functionality in a static way
- focus on the visual design

Prototype

A **high-fidelity prototype** often has a greater degree of accuracy and flowing of real content, in addition to interactive functions. This would be used for a more formal evaluation and testing before final development. Testing the final prototype is as important as the prototype design itself. Overall, prototyping will save time and aggravation with both design and development.

High-fidelity prototypes are computer-based, and usually allow realistic (mouse-keyboard) user interactions. High-fidelity prototypes are closer to a true representation of the user interface. These are especially effective in demonstrating actual products to clients.

Mid-fidelity mockups of an application, *Roc Doc,* by Yue Liu.

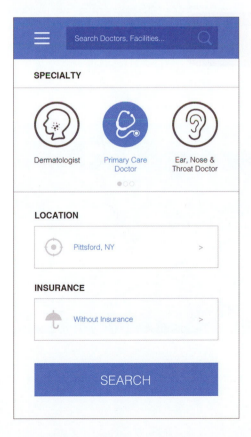

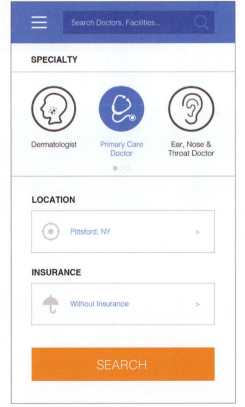

Call-To-Action

A **call-to-action** in UI /UX design refers to the elements on an app, web page, or other user interface that solicit an action from the user. Clickable items (buttons, words, images) perform an action when the user enables them. Action verbs should be used for instruction.

There is usually a visual aspect that calls the user's attention to entice them to click. Color, size, and flashing can be integrated. Buttons indicating "Order now!" or "Download Now" or "Learn More" may use color, size, and/ or flashing to indicate the call to action. Images might flash with an arrow indicating for you to click on it. A call to action desires a response from the user.

Buttons and a banner ad incorporating a call to action.

Eye Tracking

Eye tracking is a technique that can help **identify user behaviors**. When you evaluate where the user is spending the most time viewing areas of a UI, you will understand human behavior, enhance computer interaction design, and improve user interfaces.

Eye tracking involves measuring where the eye is focused or the motion of the eye as an individual views a web page.

Eye tracking aspects beneficial to user interface design:

- Eye tracking measures:
  - ◊ Gaze direction and gaze point
  - ◊ Eye movement and patterns
  - ◊ Pupil size and pupil dilation
- Where the user is looking
- How long the user is looking
- How the user is navigating the page
- What areas of the interface are missed
- How focus moves from one area to another on the page
- How size, placement, and hierarchy of items affects user attention

For more information on eye tracking, consider reading:

Eye Tracking in User Experience Design
by Jennifer Romano Bergstrom
and Andrew Schall

How to Conduct Eyetracking Studies
by Jakob Nielsen and Kara Pernice

Page Fold

The **page fold** in digital content refers to the lowest area where information is no longer visible on the screen. The position of the fold is, of course, defined by the screen resolution and the digital device. The region above the fold – often called **screenful** – describes the region of a page that is visible without scrolling. Navigation and primary feature areas must appear above the fold.

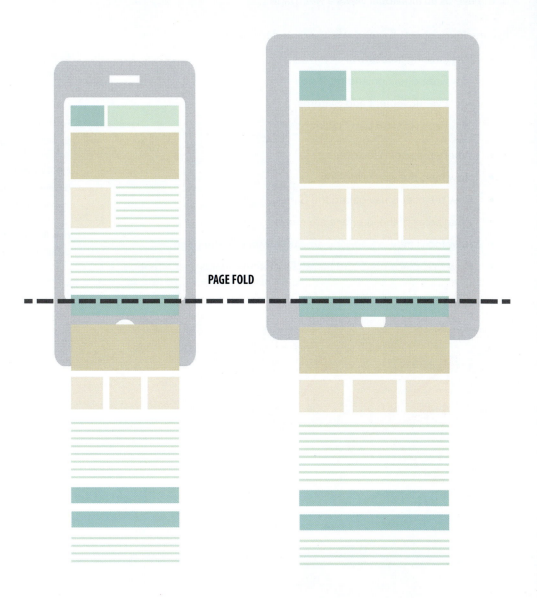

PAGE FOLD

App Design Principles

- Integrate subtle effects that contribute to a pleasant user experience.

- Use objects as buttons for emotional satisfaction and memorability.

- Allow users to add personal customization.

- Have previous choices available.

- Keep it simple and brief; use short phrases and words, rather than long sentences.

- Images can grab user attention and can be more efficient and faster than words.

- Make the most important actions easy to find and use.

- Limit the number of choices and allow user to "undo."

- Visual distinction allows the user to discern functional differences.

- Make the app easy to learn by using visual patterns and usage memory from other apps.

- Save settings and allow cross-device access for these.

- Break information and tasks into digestible chunks. Don't overwhelm the user.

- Integrate breadcrumbs and feedback so the user knows where they are and what they have accomplished.

- Allow for user mistakes and make friendly prompts for corrections .

- Enable the user to have a sense of control.

A helpful online resource:

www.usability.gov/

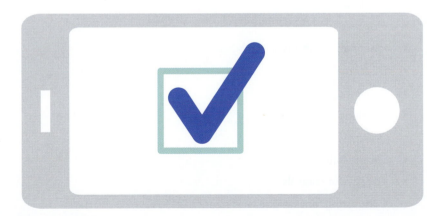

UI Design Patterns

UI design patterns provide solutions to common user interface problems. In short, design patterns are solutions to recurring design problems. Design patterns are a best practice that can be integrated into all your interactive projects.

Well-organized navigation, drag-and-drop options, blank-slate default screens, progress indicators, actionable items, social network access, search and login options, and grouping related items are just some of the UI patterns that can be incorporated.

Common UI design patterns:

- Input
- Navigation
- Data
- Tables
- Social
- Cognition
- Perception and memory
- Feedback
- Auto focus
- Drag and drop
- Auto save
- Breadcrumbs
- Blank slate
- Progress indicators
- Identifiable buttons
- Direct manipulation
- Grouping like items
- Continuous scrolling
- Glance-view dashboard
- Escape hatch
- Error proof controls
- Contrasting font weights and size

To keep the user engaged and not frustrated, design apps that behave in a consistent and predictable fashion.

Similarities & Differences between the Apple iOS and Android UI/UX Platforms

	iOS	Android
SIMILARITIES		
Environment		
Basic UI elements	X	X
Information structure	X	X
List-based navigation	X	X
Gesture controls	X	X
DIFFERENCES		
Navigation		
Top navigation	X	
Bottom navigation		X
Back navigation		
Upper Left – navigates within app	X	X
Bottom Left – navigates within device		X
Search		
Search bar at top of screen	X	
Search bar anywhere, but usually on top		X
Data Views		
Divided segment bar at top of screen	X	
Spinner with drop-down menu at top		X
Actions for Accessing Open Apps		
Stacked windows		X
Swipe left and right	X	

Ideation Tools

There is a variety of software and apps for composing layout ideas for your interactive prototypes. Below is partial list of the some of the current software and apps available for composing and developing your concepts.

The tables provide some suggested software and apps for prototyping. The designation of desktop, mobile, tablet, watch indicate the devices for which you can design with the listed products.

Software	Desktop	Mobile	Tablet	Watch
Illustrator	X	X	X	X
InDesign	X	X	X	X
Photoshop	X	X	X	X

Apps	Desktop	Mobile	Tablet	Watch
Adobe XD	X	X	X	X
Atomic	X	X	X	X
Axure RP	X	X	X	X
Briefs	X	X	X	X
Flinto	X	X	X	
FluidUI	X	X	X	X
InVision	X	X	X	
iRise	X	X	X	X
OmniGraffle	X	X	X	
Origami	X	X	X	X
Pencil	X	X	X	
Pixate	X	X	X	X
POP	X	X	X	
Proto.io	X	X	X	X
Solidify	X	X	X	

Chapter Case Study:
Creating a User Interface Prototype

For this chapter exercise, the process of prototyping for an iPhone app is presented. Development of the concept and user interface show the stages of refinement of the visual concept and user experience.

There are no exercise files to download for this chapter. You can review the project presented to gain insight on the process of prototyping. The following project was designed by Ninglin Jiang, a graduate student in the MFA Visual Communication Design program at the Rochester Institute of Technology.

The title of Ninglin's project is an Info Guide & Event Planner App, which focuses on designing a UX experience that uses interaction. The app helps visitors plan a trip to the Seneca Park Zoo. This would allow them to plan their visit, obtain info on rates and hours, plan a tour of the animals on display, and create a schedule.

Part 1: Defining the Project

The objectives of **Zoo Info Guide & Event Planner:**

- Allow users to plan their visit in advance.
- Customize their tour at the zoo.
- Make reservations and/or purchase tickets.

Part 2: Project Analysis

Once the problem/need was identified, analysis and planning began. The project was an initial concept and development of screen designs with basic interaction, enabling the designer to go through the process of developing an interactive project. This is not a fully realized app, but a design prototype. The UX process was followed in designing the app.

- **Research** – initial research helped to identify the type of mobile app that needed to be addressed. Comparative analysis of other zoo apps was conducted and referenced.
- **Demographics/Personas** – the intended audience/user for the app is parents, tourists, and zoo supporters.
- **Content** – the content was outlined and a flowchart developed. This helped to organize the content, establish sections, screens needed, and flow of the interaction.

UX Design Process

- Observe how people do things
- Brainstorm user needs
- Develop personas
- Conduct a competitive analysis
- Define information architecture
- Develop the interactive prototype
- Conduct usability testing

Part 3: Sketching and Wireframes

Ideation and **rough sketches** were developed. Variations were tried and narrowed down in order to develop a low-fidelity wireframe. The **wireframes** were shown to users for feedback on organization, flow, and content.

The wireframes were designed for a **mobile app** to run on an iPhone. Interaction scenarios were developed, allowing for evaluating user actions and finalizing content that would need to be viewed on the screen.

For more information on evaluation and testing methods, refer to Chapter 10 of this book.

Preliminary sketch of a flowchart, with final version below. Flowcharts are mandatory for content organization.

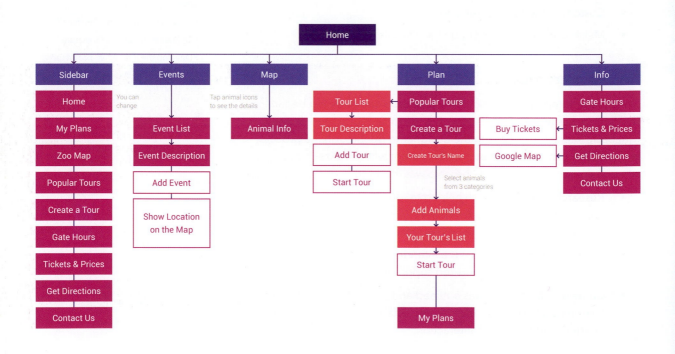

Early concept brainstorming for information architecture and site content development.

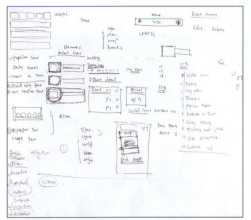

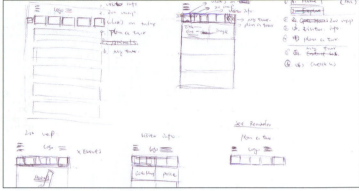

Low- to mid-fidelity wireframes.

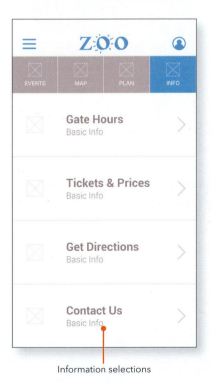

Information selections

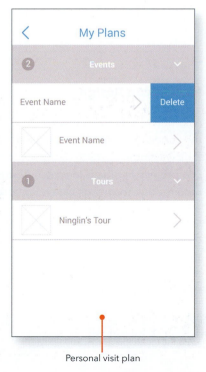

Personal visit plan

Tour selections

Part 4: Low- to Mid-Fidelity Mockups

Content, text, headings, color, visual organization, and user navigation were evaluated. After receiving feedback from the users on the low- to mid-fidelity wireframes, revisions were integrated, then evaluated one more time before a **high-fidelity prototype** was generated.

A base grid was developed to organize the content on the screen. Grids help to maintain continuity of the design.

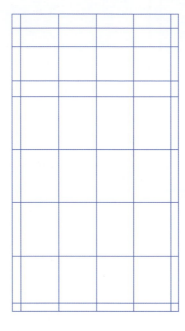

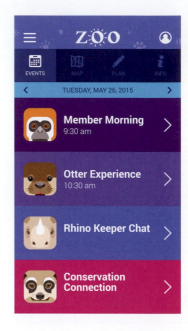

Part 5: Icon Design

A complete set of 25 icons was designed to represent the animals at the Seneca Park Zoo. Ninglin used these for both the app design and for a wayfinding system design concept developed for the Seneca Park Zoo project. In regard to screen design for multiple devices, **icon design** requires that the images are adaptable to use at various sizes.

Design principles of form, shape, line, balance, repetition, unity, common contour, and similarity were integrated. Unique aspects of each animal were addressed and simplified for easy recognition. A cohesive design through effective use of the design principles, color palette, and attention to adaptability make this a successful set of icons.

Vector sketch of icons showing use of a grid.

African
Elephant

Polar Bear

American
Alligator

African
Spurred
Tortoise

Bornean
Orangutan

Amur Tiger

Goat

Canada Lynx

Mexican
Gray Wolf

Meerkat

California
Sea Lion

Lion

Olive
Baboon

White
Rhino

Primates

Snow
Leopard

North American
River Otter

Burmese
Python

Bald
Eagle

African
Black-footed
Penguin

Spotted
Hyena

King
Vulture

Sandhill
Crane

Complete set of icons for the zoo app
by Ninglin Jiang.

- Used a "square" concept, so each
  animal's face would fit into the
  square format.
- Used the real animal's photograph
  as a reference to capture their
  unique characteristics.
- Used "axial symmetry" method
  in design.

Part 6: Final Prototype Design

The final prototype was evaluated on two levels:

- **Visual interface:** Overall content and visual organization, color, typography, and imagery.

- **Interaction:** The prototype was put into a testing app. This allowed for evaluating user responses to the interactivity. In this case, Invision was used (www.invisonapp.com) for the final **high-fidelity prototype.**

You can download screen templates for all devices, for example:

www.sketchappsources.com

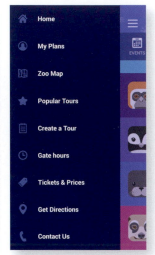

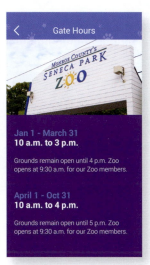

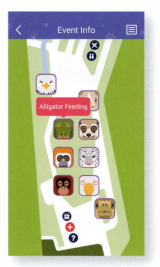

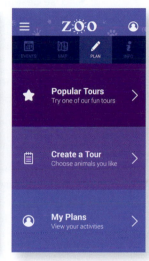

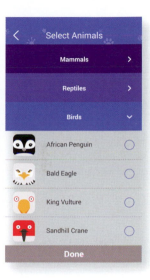

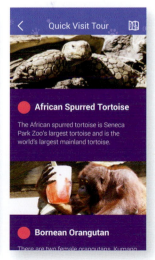

A selection of the screen designs for the **Zoo Info Guide & Event Planner** app prototype.

Summary

Designing a successful prototype for an interactive UX requires understanding visual design and interaction principles as related to the user. From sketch to prototype, a combination of technical workflow, user testing, and design principles are integrated. Knowing your user, the content, and the method of digital delivery and devices will aid in creating effective user interface prototypes.

Key principles that the designer should follow are:

- Use design principles when developing an interface design
- Always keep the user in mind
- Evaluate and test to gain feedback throughout the design

This completes the chapter on prototyping a user interface design. You should now be able to:

- Integrate design thinking, ideation, and sketching
- Apply visual design principles to an interface design
- Understand the process of planning and designing an effective user interface design through prototyping

The next chapter focuses on designing interactions.

The Big Picture:
User Experience (UX) Design

4

Designing Interactions

Interaction design (IxD) is not just about clicking on, or tapping buttons to navigate to different screens. It encompasses a wide spectrum, most importantly – human factors. Understanding how humans think, process information, and behave is critical to creating engaging interactive experiences between people and devices. Designers need to focus on interactivity, where the user controls the sequence and the pace of the content delivered at any given time.

This chapter explores interaction and user experience design in action. At the completion of this chapter, you will be able to:

- Discuss the components of user experience design.

- Apply principles of interaction design to projects.

- Describe principles and "laws" of interaction design.

- Discuss how mental models influence conceptual models for different types of user engagement.

- Design an interactive app for a smartphone.

The Big Picture:
User Experience (UX) Design

Interaction design (IxD) focuses on how the project works to meet the user's needs. This is an iterative process where potential solutions are tested to guide the designer in building the best possible user experience. An important concept to remember is that usability testing is not user experience design. Why? Usability testing focuses on how easy the interactivity was in allowing users to complete their tasks.

Users can access content in an increasing number of ways from the Web, to mobile apps, to wearable devices. In the past, interaction design focused more on the aesthetics, with little to no thought about how the users would feel as they interacted with the final project. That has changed in recent years due to the ubiquitous nature of the Web and advancements in mobile technology. So, what is user experience design?

User experience (UX) design includes several design processes to determine how efficient and pleasant the experience was for the users.

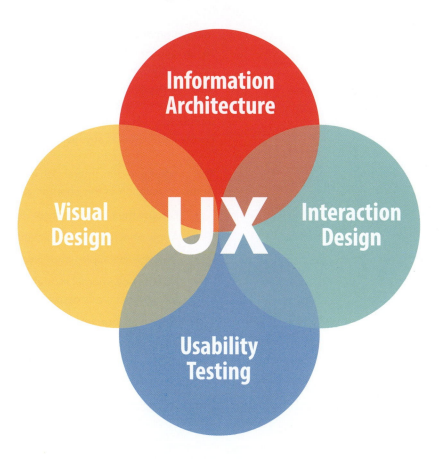

Chapter 4 | Designing Interactions

User experience design (UX) focuses on how useful and/or enjoyable the overall final interaction was to the user. It is all about how the user feels when interacting with a system, no matter what device is used. User experience design includes several design processes to determine how efficient and pleasant the experience was for the users.

For digital design, these processes include the following:

- **Information Architecture** determines the content, its priority, and where and when it will appear in the final project.
- **Visual Design** facilitates the communication of content and how the user processes it on any given screen.
- **Interaction Design** establishes the methods for how the user controls the content.
- **Usability Testing** determines how the performance of the interactions met the user's needs and goals.

Designing Interactions

As a component of user experience design, interaction design puts the user in control of the content. You must anticipate how someone might interact with the system, anticipate errors that could occur, as well as build engaging interfaces that meet user expectations.

When approaching adding interactivity to a project, consider the person who will be using your project, and the context in which the project might be used. Ask the following questions:

- **How will the user interact?** Users can interact with content on a device through various methods including clicking/tapping, entering information, dragging, and swiping.
- **What input device will be used?** Think about the various input devices including the mouse, finger, stylus, or keyboard. Direct manipulation mimics touching a similar object in the physical world and is more easily learned and used. Indirect manipulation alters an object through other means such as menus or keyboard shortcuts.
- **Which visual clues help the user understand what to interact with?** Color, shape, and size help the user distinguish what is clickable and what isn't. If a button does not look like a button, the user may not see it. Also think about multiple senses that go beyond point-and-click, such as voice and gestures.

For further readings on interaction design and its principles, try ***Designing for Interaction*** by Dan Saffer.

For further readings on interaction design and user experience design, read *Seductive Interaction Design: Creating Playful, Fun, and Effective User Experiences (Voices That Matter)* by Stephen P. Anderson.

- **How is the user informed about what will happen?** Users have perceived expectations when clicking or tapping on a button. Reinforce their action by telling them the resulting outcome through meaningful button labels and clear instructions. This reduces user trial and error, or failure to complete the interaction.

- **What acknowledgment is given to the user's action?** Users need to see some form of response that informs them that their actions were "heard" by the system. Let the users know what is happening.

- **When is visual feedback required for the response time?** If a system process lasts longer that two seconds, visual feedback is required. This could take the form of an hourglass, text, or a progress indicator displaying the time still required to complete the action.

- **What constraints are put in place that limit or prevent errors?** Error messages help explain why the error occurred and provide a way for the user to recover from the problem.

- **How do users know where they are and how they got there?** User orientation shows users the lay of the land, how to travel, where they currently are on the map, and where they have visited in the past. A simple change in a button's color and a "breadcrumb" list of links illustrates the user's journey.

Ask yourself how the user will interact with the content, and how the system will respond to the user's actions in a timely manner.

INPUT

FEEDBACK

ERRORS

DEVICE

TIME

Focus on Perceived Affordance

How does a shape imply functionality? Don Norman, cofounder of the Nielsen Norman Group, introduced the concept of **affordances** to the interaction design field. Affordances deal with properties that provide some indication of how to interact with an object. Scissors are a common example used to illustrate the concept of affordance due to its simplicity in design. How do scissors relate to interaction design for the screen?

Interactive elements that look like physical objects or user interfaces that mimic a real environment can enhance a project's usability. Think about the icons used in the Macintosh iOS operating system. Folders store your content. A trash can deletes files from your computer. You instinctively know how to use these items based on how they function in the world.

An affordance connects the visual elements to other things or actions that the user is familiar with. It is the visual clues that suggest meaning through words, shapes, color, or movement. Users look for something to click or tap. Adding three-dimensional properties to the button implies that it can be pushed. If it looks like a button, it probably is a button. As a result, the user will click or tap it based on its appearance.

The Nielsen Norman Group provides many articles on their research and evaluations of user interface designs at *www.nngroup.com*.

An object's shape provides users with clues on how to interact with it.

The button's appearance: its shading, drop shadow, and highlights suggest that it can be clicked or tapped. Color can also suggest the function's outcome when the user interacts with it – red equals danger or caution.

Show Me the Interactions

You need to understand how affordance works in order to make your designs easier to use and to quickly direct the users' actions on what you want them to do. The effectiveness of a perceived affordance depends upon its appearance. These visual clues come in different types, each serving different purposes.

An **explicit affordance** clearly tells the user how to interact with an object through text and visual appearance. Upon first glance the users can guess at how to interact with the object. This type works well for users who are not tech-savvy or who do not regularly interact with on-screen interfaces. However, too much explicit instruction can create redundancy or be condescending to users.

A call-to-action button is a good example of an explicit affordance. The text, "Download the App," provides the simplest way to convey that information. It is always best to keep the language simple and clear.

A **pattern affordance** adheres to common interaction trends that tech-savvy users should easily recognize or know. For example, any blue text that is underlined implies a hyperlink. If the users click on the company's logo, they will be transported back to the site's home page. A strip of words across the top of the screen suggests a navigation menu. It is the user's familiarity with the pattern that makes the affordance effective.

An input text field with a magnifying glass icon suggests search capabilities. Text links are traditionally colored blue and underlined. These are so common on most sites that they have become established patterns for interactivity.

The term affordance was introduced to human-computer interaction by Donald Norman in his book *The Psychology of Everyday Things*.

A **hidden affordance** is only revealed once a certain condition has been met. For example, a object that changes in color when moused over suggests a link that could be clicked. These are often used to simplify complex interfaces by establishing a form of interactive hierarchy. Use a hidden affordance for any secondary actions so that it does not compete with vital interactions, or to de-clutter the screen of interactive elements. The only issue is that the users need to find them because they are initially hidden. If the interaction is vital to the user; do not hide it.

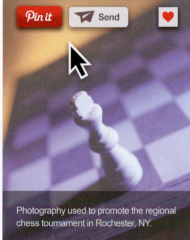

Photography used to promote the regional chess tournament in Rochester, NY.

Pinterest is a good example of using hidden affordance. Options to Pin, Send, and Like a photo appear only when the user hovers over an image.

A **negative affordance** displays a feature that is not available, at least not at the moment. It is equally important to show and tell the user what he/she can and cannot do with the interface. The most common visual clue is grayed-out text or buttons. This allows the user to effectively scan for active options using color and contrast.

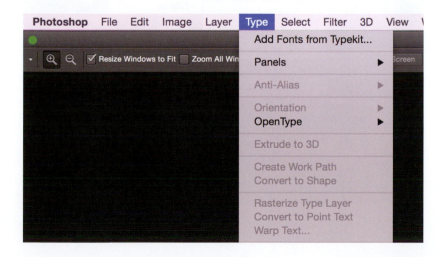

For menu options, the gray text fades into the background while the black text stands out and reads as clickable.

According to Fitts's Law, the target width of a button needs to be large enough for the user to click or tap on.

Interaction Laws

Take a look at the smartphone UI mockup to the left. Is the LOGIN button a reasonable size to tap? Introduced by Paul Fitts in 1954, **Fitts's Law** states that an interactive element needs to be big enough for a user to click it. Larger objects are always easier to interact with. This is particularly important in a mobile context that has a touch component.

Fitts's Law also encourages placement of buttons and menus at the edges or corners of the screen as they provide a boundary that a cursor cannot go beyond. As a result, the probability of interacting with the item increases. Look at the menu system in any Adobe software application.

In addition to the size and position of an interactive element, Fitts's Law also addressed the time it takes to move from a starting position to the final target. In some cases, a pop-up menu that appears where the user clicked is faster than having the user move the cursor up to the header and select the drop-down menu.

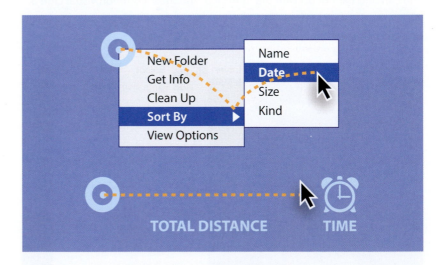

An action should always happen close to where the interaction occurs.

George Miller, a cognitive psychologist, found that people are only able to keep five to nine items in their short-term memory before they forget or make errors. This is referred to as **Miller's Law** or the **Magical Number Seven** rule. This does not mean that you are limited to only providing seven menu items or seven buttons to click on. Miller's Law suggests that designers should "chunk" information and actions into meaningful groups for users to focus on, process, retain, and recall.

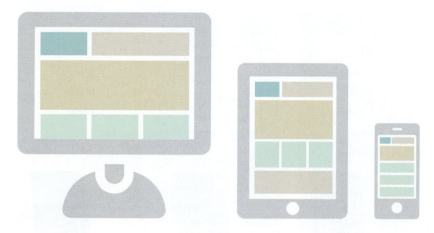

"Chunking" content and actions allows users to retain and recall information more easily, especially for e-learning projects and responsive web design.

Tesler's Law of Conservation of Complexity suggests removing as much complexity as possible from the user. With that said, he also noted to keep in mind that things can only be simplified to a certain point before they no longer function. Take a look at the dialog box below, the interaction cannot be simplified any more without causing confusion and possibly user error.

Larry Teslar is a pioneer in interaction design and has worked at Xerox PARC, Apple, Amazon, and Yahoo!.

Hick's Law also deals with time and is related to Miller's Law regarding short-term memory. Essentially the law states that the time it takes for a user to make a decision is based on the number of available choices. The decision time is also affected by how familiar a format is to follow and how familiar the user is with the choices. The example below provides a couple of options for simplifying a simple selection task. Always focus on how a user will interact with an application or a website.

An average user expects and requires simple interactions to complete their task. There are several ways to simplify the number of choices for the user.

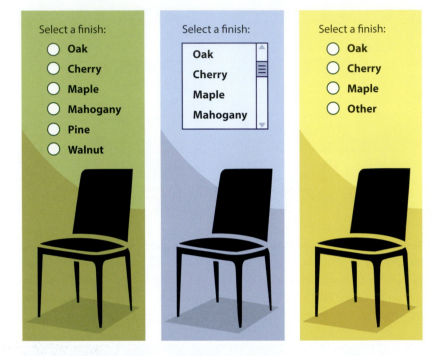

Select a finish:
- Oak
- Cherry
- Maple
- Mahogany
- Pine
- Walnut

Select a finish:
Oak
Cherry
Maple
Mahogany

Select a finish:
- Oak
- Cherry
- Maple
- Other

For further readings on mental models, read *Mental Models: Aligning Design Strategy with Human Behavior* by Indie Young.

Human Behavior and Interaction Design

A designer's goal is to engage their users by anticipating how they think, how they process information, and how they will behave. Users learn from their past experiences, generalize them, and transfer what they learned to new experiences. This thought process is referred to as a **mental model**.

When we encounter a new situation, we turn to our mental model and look for similarities with our previous experiences. We process information, make decisions, and solve problems based on our memory, recognition, and the associations we have acquired. Mental models influence the **conceptual model**, which defines the appearance of the final design and how it works to the user.

The first steps in formulating a conceptual model include asking:

- What controls will the users have to view the content?
- How will the system respond to the user's action?
- What kind of visual metaphor, if any, is appropriate?

Image Maps versus Visual Metaphors

Interacting with content can be achieved using an image map system or through the use of a visual metaphor. **Image maps** consist of visual elements that literally represent, and navigate to, the content. These visuals can be a series of images or icons, with or without supporting text. The user clicks or taps on an image to learn more about the topic associated with it.

A **metaphor** integrates the concept of an image map into an activity, object, or environment that the user can relate to. It allows easier access to a complex system by presenting information in terms of an object (book), a location (office), or a device (DVD/Blu-ray player) that the user is already familiar with and uses outside the digital environment.

In order for the metaphor to work, it needs to be appropriate for the content and relatable to the user. Metaphors create meaning for the content. If a user has to ask what the meaning is, the metaphor is not working. The benefits of visual metaphors is to make learning a new system easier and more accessible to users.

Users recall and apply their closest past experiences to new digital experiences. An EPUB is a good example of taking the concept of a traditional book and translating its interactivity online. Figure out your target user's closest experience.

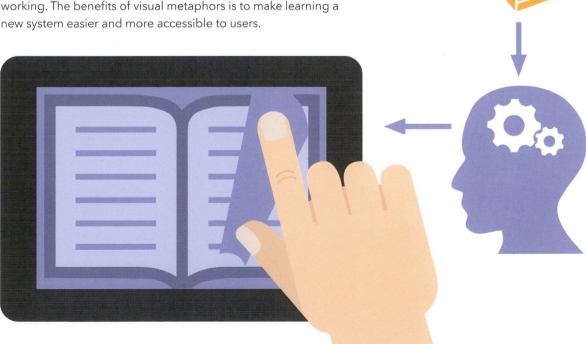

Types of Interactions

The goal is to get users doing something quickly. People learn best when they are actively engaged. When designing interactions, the user, not the computer, initiates and controls all actions.

There are several interaction types. These include:

- **Direct Manipulation:** The user physically interacts with objects in a virtual or physical space by clicking or tapping on them with an input device. The final design needs to include interactive objects that provide immediate feedback to the user's actions.

- **Indirect Manipulation:** The user tells the system to do something through commands such as save and print. The final design needs to support the user issuing commands and selecting options through menus and keyboard shortcuts.

- **Conversation:** Advancements in technology now allow users to interact with a device using speech, such as Siri on the Apple iPhone. The device has to be ready to receive voice commands and special attention must be addressed regarding the user's environment, specifically public spaces.

- **Physical Motion:** Hand-eye coordination is predominantly thought of when it comes to interaction design. Devices can also track human motion through a Global Positioning System (GPS) or built-in motion sensors, such as the Sony Kinect, Nintendo Wii, and the Leap Motion controllers. Selecting the best gesture needs to be determined based on the device and the physical environment.

For further readings on interaction design, read *Interdisciplinary Interaction Design: A Visual Guide to Basic Theories, Models and Ideas for Thinking and Designing* by James Pannafino.

Put the user in control using direct manipulation such as tapping, indirect manipulation through the use of a menu system, speech, and/or gestures.

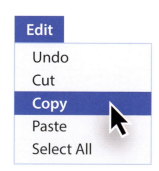

Which type of interaction is best? That all depends on the user's task:

- **Clicking, tapping, dragging, and swiping** are good for actions, such as selecting, moving, drawing, building, etc.
- **Menus and keyboard shortcuts** are good for repetitive tasks such as navigation and file management. Users must be informed of any shortcut key combinations, whereas menus allow the user to immediately begin using the system.
- **Voice interaction** is often good for young children, disabled users. and specialized voice-controlled devices.
- **Gestures and body movement** are used in online gaming and for more physical activities.

Putting the User at Ease and in Control

Typically, a user asks the following questions when presented with a system to interact with:

- **What can I do?** Ensure functions are visible to the user.
- **How can I get to where I want to go?** Make the most important functions the easiest to find. In some cases, simplify or limit the number of actions that can be performed at one time.
- **Where have I been?** Use elements of visual design, such as color and contrast, to highlight the user's journey.
- **What have I done?** Be consistent in the use of available features.
- **What is the system doing now?** Feedback from the system is crucial to let the user know what effect their actions have had.

For further readings on interaction design and user experience design, read **_User-Centered Design_** by Travis Lowdermilk.

Graphical breadcrumbs show the user's location in the project's hierarchical structure. If the user has to follow a linear path, use color to highlight the journey. Finally, a progress control needs to provide visual feedback that a system operation is underway.

It is important that users feel in control at all times when interacting with a system. If the users feel comfortable with the interactivity, they will trust that the system will protect them from making errors. Trust inspires confidence, and with confidence the user engagement will increase as users delve deeper into the online experience.

Types of Interactive Controls

How the user engages a system, such as clicking, tapping, talking, or gesturing, impacts the kind of interaction needed. There are many kinds of interface control types available, each serving a specific type of interaction:

- **Buttons:** Use for actions such as navigation or submitting data.
- **Check boxes:** Use for selections and turning an option on or off.
- **Dials and sliders:** Use to input numeric ranges.
- **Text fields:** Use for inputting data into forms or search areas.
- **Text areas:** Use for user comments and feedback.

Buttons, check boxes, sliders, and text fields allow the user to control the content.

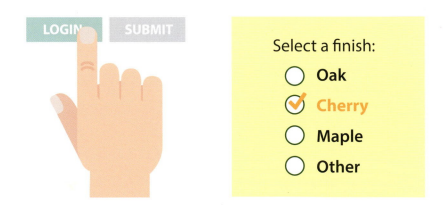

Reduce User Errors

As mentioned previously, a designer's goal is to engage their users by anticipating how they think. To prevent or limit user errors, try to forecast as many as possible mistakes that the user could make. If an error cannot be completely eliminated, build in feedback to help users recover from the error quickly and without disrupting their engagement.

User errors can be prevented by:

- Designing interactions consistently that will promote predictability and improve the overall learnability of the site

- Providing clear descriptive instructions

- Avoiding text input that relies on correct spelling

- Disabling functions that aren't relevant to the user's task at hand

- Offer alternative methods to accommodate users with different levels of experience

- Changing the visual state of an object or item as a result of the user's actions

- Providing a "back," "undo," or "cancel" button or command to recover from any mistakes made

- Offering clear warning messages to exit paths that may irreversibly impact the user's data and journey through the content

For further readings on interaction design, read *Interaction Design: Beyond Human-Computer Interaction* by Jenny Preece, Helen Sharp, and Yvonne Rogers.

Design pop-up warnings as a way to prevent user errors. This makes users think about what they're doing, explains what will happen as a result of their actions, and provides interactive controls for confirmation.

Chapter Case Study:
Designing Interactions for a Mobile App

For this chapter exercise, let's apply the interaction laws and design techniques discussed so far to create an app for a smartphone. For this assignment, the application needs to leverage user experience methodologies to quantify smartphone usage. The goal is to make users aware of the amount of time they spend using their devices.

There are no exercise files to download for this chapter. You can follow along with the example shown, or experiment and create your own design. The following project was designed by Tejal Sampat, a graduate student in the MFA Visual Communication Design program at the Rochester Institute of Technology.

Users select an emoji to express their emotions. They can choose from six moods: frustration, worried, boredom, rolling eyes, anxiety, and anger.

The title of Tejal's project is **timeOut** which addresses the issue of being neglected in social situations. The mobile application allows neglected users to send anonymous timeouts to obsessive smartphone users, who are preoccupied with their smartphones and are in close proximity to the neglected users. The goal of the project is to influence behavior through nudges, prompts, and challenges that help the users in making positive behavioral changes.

Part 1: Defining the Context and Content

As discussed in Chapter 1, context answers who, what, when, where, how, and for what purpose. Content refers to the actual intellectual message to be communicated. A mind map for the **timeOut** project was developed to visually represent ideas and information.

The goal was to combine design with technology and figure out how they can be used in reducing smartphone addiction. Various methods like haptic, voice, location, and gesture-based notifications were researched. User habits were studied to determine the most frequently performed tasks.

The **timeOut** mobile application had the following objectives:

- To positively influence social behavior and impact smartphone usage with the help of a user-friendly interface
- To promote conversation
- To make obsessive smartphone users aware of their distractive social behavior

Part 2: Determining the Users and Their Tasks

Next, define the intended audience and how they will engage with the content. It is important to design user work flows and understand user needs. A workflow diagram depicts a series of actions that describe the task at hand. It visualizes the task stream and the actions required by the user to navigate the application.

Two unique users were identified for the **timeOut** mobile application:

- Individuals that would like their phone-obsessed friends to halt their device addiction in social situations
- Users addicted to their smartphones

A mind map is a diagram used to visually organize your thoughts regarding a project's context and content to be communicated.

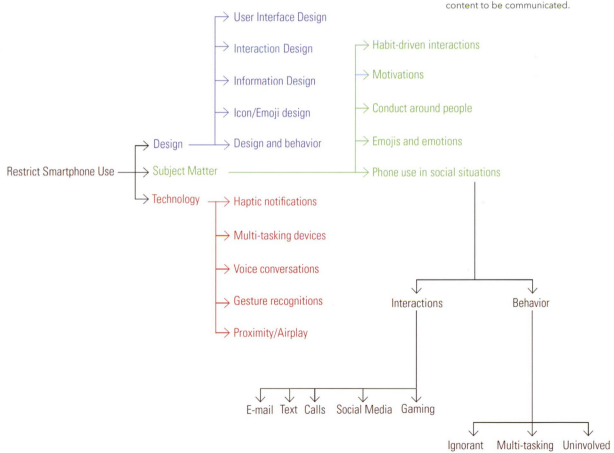

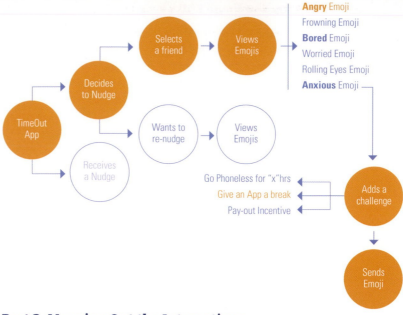

The workflow diagram for the responsible user depicts the tasks required to send a nudge to the obsessive smartphone user.

Part 3: Mapping Out the Interactions

One of the primary goals of the **timeOut** application was the ease with which a user could send emojis, therefore a lot of effort was put into creating the wireframes. Since this is a mobile application, it is important to visually indicate the hand gestures on the wireframes. Different gesturing methods were tested to determine the most efficient method of interaction.

The wireframes were designed to determine the types of interactions needed and create simplicity for the user.

Once a challenge has been sent, the emoji takes over the obsessive user's screen and they are made aware of their behavior. Next, they have an option to accept a challenge or wait a few seconds and decline. Once they accept the challenge, the app tracks their usage and notifies them when they try to give up on the challenge.

Part 4: Branding the Visual Design

This step involves brand and vision creation for your application. Keep the target audience in mind when you choose your color palette. The prioritization of colors hints at the importance of creating a user-friendly interface/experience. In the **timeOut** mobile application, the cooler shades of blue represent boredom and annoyance, whereas the warmer colors depict anger and anxiety. The base color yellow-orange represents attentiveness.

Yellow - Represents concentration/attention

Blues - Represent bored/annoyed/tired

The **timeOut** color palette helps establish the overall visual brand.

Reds - Represent anger/agitation/frustration

Various design styles and resources were explored for the **timeOut** logo. The final design contains the mood slider, a blue time ticker, and the top view of a cup of coffee. The slider represents the change in mood (internally consistent with the app) and the logo name "timeOut."

The inspiration for the logo included friends chitchatting, social gatherings, a timer, time running out, a clock ticking, and a cup of coffee.

Apple provides iOS Human Interface Guidelines at *https://developer.apple. com/library/ios/documentation/ UserExperience/Conceptual/ MobileHIG/*.

Conception of preliminary visual design was the main focus of this step. The iOS and Android guidelines were studied to ensure that the designed application was internally and externally consistent. This process involved defining the UI elements as well as interactivity for various features.

Part 5: Prototyping the Interactions

Once the designs are finalized, it is important to build the interactions to bring the project to life. A prototype is used to demonstrate the overall user experience and interactions of the project. This allows for review and testing of the navigation and layout, as well as the application from a holistic point of view.

User help and control is provided through buttons.

User orientation is provided to show progression.

User instructions help reduce user errors.

These screenshots are from a four-step walkthrough that was designed to allow users to better understand the application and its features.

The grayed-out interface is a negative affordance as it displays features that are not available during the walkthrough.

Hick's Law simplifies the selection task so that the user is not overwhelmed by a lot of choices all at once.

The magnifying glass is a pattern affordance that users should easily recognize or know.

Design for the device. The position of the app's buttons is in relationship to the phone's keyboard.

These screenshots show how the user must first choose a person to send a timeout to. They can choose a person from their smartphone contacts or use the search function to look for friends.

These screenshots show how the user selects an emoji to express their emotions to their obsessive smartphone friend.

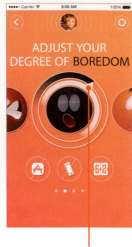

Consistency in the placement and shape of the buttons helps the user learn the system.

User orientation is provided to show a user's progression.

Dials and sliders assist the user in inputting numeric ranges and levels.

These screenshots show how the user can add a challenge to their timeout to motivate their friends to put down their phones. Users have three unique challenges to choose from.

Fitts's Law encourages the placement of buttons at the edges of the screen. The probability of interacting with the item increases.

Provide a "back" button or command for the user to recover from any mistakes.

Graphical breadcrumbs and button highlights show the user's location in the hierarchical structure.

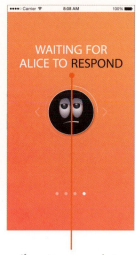

These screenshots show how the user can review their timeout, adjust the duration, and swipe to send it to their phone-addicted friend.

Offer alternative methods to accommodate users with different levels of experience. Uses can click the button or swipe up on the emoji.

If a system process lasts longer that 2 seconds, visual feedback is required.

Feedback from the app is crucial to let the user know what effect their actions have had.

The phone-addicted friend receives a visual notification of the timeout and challenge. They can accept the challenge or wait 15 seconds to decline. This interactive proof-of-concept was built with the prototyping tool **Axure**. The assets were taken from the high-fidelity designs and exported as individual images. The interactive prototype provided an effective way to demonstrate the complex interactions to users.

The phone-addicted friend receives a visual notification of the timeout and the challenge.

Summary

Users want interactions to be easy to use, have quick response times, and not require too much thinking. To achieve this, designers should research human behavior and patterns related to software usage. For example, users have expectations about how hyperlinks are supposed to look and function on the Web. Departing from the standards can have a negative impact on the overall user experience.

This completes the chapter. You should now be able to:

- Discuss the components of user experience design.
- Apply principles of interaction design to projects.
- Describe principles and "laws" of interaction design.
- Discuss how mental models influence conceptual models for different types of user engagement.

The next chapter focuses on Responsive Web Design (RWD).

5

Exploring Responsive Design

Browsing the Web can be done across a wide range of different screen sizes: from desktops to smartphones, tablets, and even wearable devices. Websites that are not optimized and designed to work across multiple devices negatively impact the user's experience. As designers we must accept that screen sizes will always be changing and embrace the challenge to design flexible layouts that adapt to any screen size, today and in the future. This is the basic idea behind responsive design.

This chapter explores responsive design in action. At the completion of this chapter, you will be able to:

- Describe what Responsive Web Design (RWD) is and how it works.

- Apply design principles to screen layouts for mobile devices.

- Discuss mobile design patterns and best practices.

- Design an HTML layout that changes based on the screen size and capabilities of the device.

- Optimize content that responds to the needs of the users and the devices they are using.

What Is Responsive Web Design?

As more and more people use mobile devices to surf the Web, a web page's layout needs to be optimized to meet the user's needs. The user's experience on a smartphone is completely different from the desktop experience. Many websites originally designed for a desktop cannot simply be ported over to a mobile device. Why?

In the past, designers would build a website using a fixed width, typically around 960 pixels, to accommodate a large percentage of desktop users with a viewport, or screen width, of 1024 x 786 pixels.

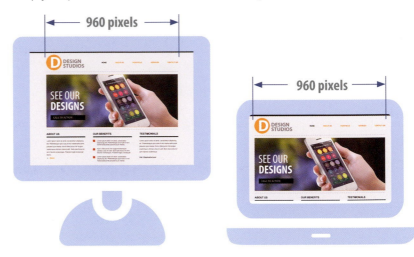

On a smartphone, a fixed-grid layout will either scale too small to be readable, or will only display a portion of the user interface making the user scroll to see more.

Traditionally, all web pages were designed using a fixed-grid layout. Content was locked into place so users experienced it in exactly the same way regardless of the screen display on which it was viewed. Even though the size of displays changed, designers had a firm grasp on creating web content at a specific screen width and resolution for a majority of users.

Chapter 5 | Exploring Responsive Design

Fixed-grid layouts are still used today. However, with the shifting trend toward mobile computing, the design approach of one-size-fits-all falls apart. A fixed-grid layout will not be as user friendly on a smaller, mobile device since the user may only see a portion of the user interface, and will need to scroll vertically and horizontally to see all the content. Whereas vertical scrolling is a widely accepted method in user navigation, horizontal scrolling is considered problematic and not as intuitive.

That is where Ethan Marcotte's **Responsive Web Design** (RWD) approach comes into play. It is a design strategy that uses a fluid grid layout that progressively adjusts to the available screen real estate on which it is displayed. It is the same HTML content, just moved, scaled, and rearranged to fit the device using CSS3 media queries. Responsive design is about rethinking design strategies and determining how users will interact with the content on different screen sizes and resolutions.

Web designer Ethan Marcotte coined the term Responsive Web Design in his online article for A List Apart in May 2010: *alistapart.com/article/ responsive-web-design.*

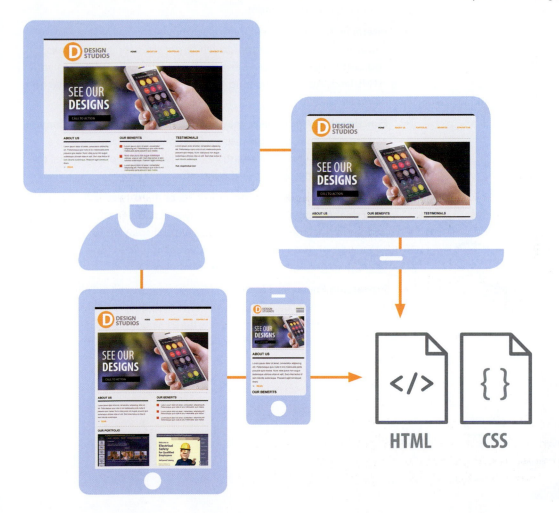

Empathize with the Mobile User

With the dramatic shift toward accessing content on devices, you must first empathize with the mobile audience. Mobile users are on the go, often need information quickly, and are more prone to distractions. Smartphones, tablets, and wearables all serve a different purpose in their lives from a desktop or a laptop computer.

Designers must know the respective limitations and capabilities of both their target user and the digital device for which they are designing. To address the needs of a mobile user, and build a compatible website for any screen, there are design challenges that need to be considered:

- **Screen Size:** A smaller screen display demands optimization of the content and design layout. Communicate only the essential information that the users need. Apply type hierarchy to enhance scannability of the content.

- **Interactivity:** A touch gesture does not have the same accuracy as a mouse click. Design bigger touch target sizes for images, links, and buttons to reduce user errors. Use CSS to add padding to your HTML links. Also keep in mind that touch-enabled devices have no hover state, only touch.

- **Functionality:** A web page may contain multiple columns of content with complex navigational menus. Streamline this content into a single-column layout for smartphones. Use accordions and lists to hide/show menu options and content.

- **Connection Speed:** A smartphone's 3G or 4G service still does not provide the same reliable connectivity as a cable modem. Since images impact the download times, avoid displaying large images or backgrounds on mobile devices. For simple icons and shapes, use CSS to generate them instead of images.

- **Processing Power and Memory:** Mobile devices still fall short in available memory and CPU power. Optimize scripted interactivity by targeting HTML elements as few times as possible. Give your elements IDs to allow JavaScript to find them quickly and efficiently.

Think about the limitations and capabilities of both your user and the digital device for which you are designing.

VIEWING CONDITIONS

CONNECTIVITY

SCREEN SIZE

DISTRACTION

Choosing the Right Design Approach

As mobile computing is on the verge of surpassing desktop and laptop usage, there are new theories and practices on how to design for a mobile world. Screen size is the key determining factor. **Desktop first** is a design strategy for building creative page layouts and interactivity for larger screens. This leaves the mobile environment secondary.

Designers start with a full, standard-size website and work their way down, removing content and functional features to fit the device's smaller screen width. This is known as **graceful degradation**. As a result, mobile websites are often shrunken, simplified versions of desktop sites.

Due to device limitations, complex websites built for desktops are not always easy to adapt to mobile devices. So where do you begin? Start with your users. If you know that a majority of the targeted audience will access the site on a mobile device, start designing there. This concept is referred to as **mobile first**.

Designers start with the most important information and interactive features for the mobile version, then add more complexity as the screen size gets bigger on tablets and desktops. This is known as **progressive enhancement**. It allows everyone to access the basic content and functionality of a web page with the addition of providing an enhanced version to those with larger screens, greater bandwidth, and CPU power.

Mobile First by Luke Wroblewski is a good resource that makes the case for why websites and applications should be designed for mobile first.

Understanding Progressive Enhancement by Aaron Gustafson is an online article on A List Apart: *alistapart.com/article/ understandingprogressiveehancement*

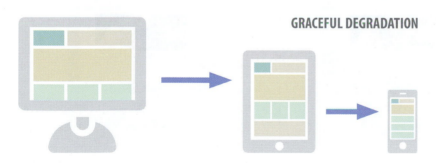

GRACEFUL DEGRADATION

PROGRESSIVE ENHANCEMENT

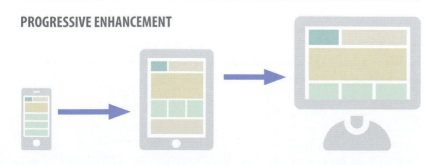

In some cases, designers create separate, mobile-optimized websites. This is referred to as **adaptive web design** and could potentially triple the time it takes to make updates. That is where responsive design is a good compromise. It uses one website and simply rearranges its appearance depending on the device. Its goal is to keep the content, functionality, and user experience intact no matter the screen width on which it is viewed.

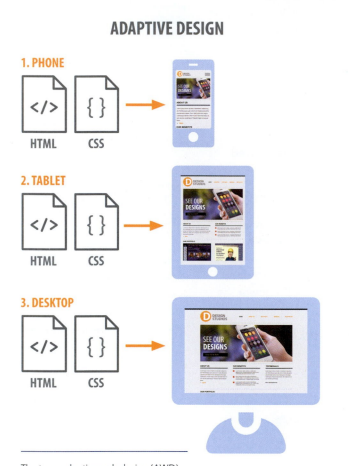

ADAPTIVE DESIGN

1. PHONE
HTML   CSS

2. TABLET
HTML   CSS

3. DESKTOP
HTML   CSS

RESPONSIVE DESIGN

1. PHONE, TABLET, DESKTOP
HTML   CSS

The term adaptive web design (AWD) was coined by author Aaron Gustafson. Adaptive web design uses a device-detection script that runs on the web server, as well as multiple versions of the site optimized for each device.

There really isn't a right or wrong way to go about responsive design. As always, designers need to keep the users' and clients' business goals in mind. Research and determine what kind of information the targeted audience is looking for. Analyze their behavioral patterns to determine whether to design for desktop first or mobile first.

Designing for a Mobile World

As you read in previous chapters, the structure of the screen's layout establishes the relationship among the individual elements, unifying them together as a whole. Unfortunately there is no standard screen size for mobile devices. Creating a single design will not work. No matter what screen size, the limited real estate afforded by a mobile device is important to keep in mind.

Use the actual content as a good starting point for designing the screen layout. Match the content to the types of content elements that will be on the web page: headers, navigation, articles, sidebars, footers, etc. When laying out your designs:

- Start with a smaller screen size and then go up

- Create a minimal composition, typically a single-column page layout, to limit scrolling to one direction

- Take into account the actual content in regard to screen widths

- Use descriptive text for quick user reading and scanning

- Increase contrast between the text and background colors and/or images

Examples of screen sizes used today:

320 x 480 = iPhone 3G
480 x 800 = Android (Medium)
560 x 960 = Android (Large)
640 x 960 = iPhone 4
640 x 1136 = iPhone 5
750 × 1334 = iPhone 6
1242 × 2208 = iPhone 6 Plus

Start designing with the actual content in mind. Match the content to the content elements on the web page.

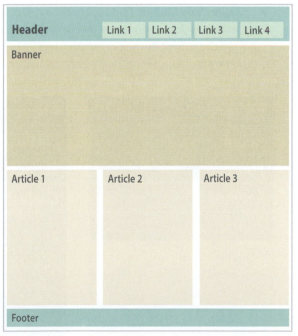

Optimizing Responsive Navigation

Navigation is a critical element for both desktop and mobile design. The goal is to keep the navigation as simple and intuitive as possible for the user to access the site. There are several methods that can be used to optimize the navigation menu for a variety of screen sizes. These include:

- **Resize and Reposition:** This approach makes on-screen navigation smaller in size and changes the padding between links using CSS. As the screen size decreases, links will typically reposition under a logo and eventually become a vertically stacked menu. This method always displays the navigation and works best for sites with few links.

- **Overlay Drop-Downs:** This approach initially hides the navigation allowing for more screen real estate for the page content. Links are provided only when the user needs them using a drop-down menu system. A menu icon indicates where the navigation is located while taking up little space in the user interface.

- **Block Drop-Downs:** This is similar to the overlay drop-down navigation menu. However, the links push down the rest of the page when they are displayed rather than appear on top of the content. Keep in mind that CSS animation requires more processing power to achieve smooth motion.

- **Sliding Side Menus:** This approach was first popularized in iOS devices. Hidden navigation menus, called "drawers," slide out from the side of the screen when a toggle switch is tapped. jQuery is often used to build this side-menu option.

A collection of responsive design patterns can be found online at *bradfrost.github.io/this-is-responsive/patterns.html.*

The hamburger icon is a classic UI element. It consists of three black bars used as a toggle switch for menus.

OVERLAY DROP-DOWN MENU

BLOCK DROP-DOWN MENU

SLIDING SIDE MENU

Creating Retina Images

With the popularity of Retina screens, consider using **high-pixel-density (HiDPI) images** in your design. How do you create these? Save a set of your images at twice the size. For example, a 200 x 200 pixel image would become 400 x 400 pixels. Save the two graphics using the same name for both, but add "2x" at the end of the Retina images file name. These images are then displayed in the original image size dimensions to create a crisp appearance on Retina screens.

A good resource for understanding how to design for Retina displays is *sebastien-gabriel.com/designers-guide-to-dpi.*

NORMAL IMAGE (1x)
200 x 200 pixels

RETINA IMAGE (2x)
400 x 400 pixels

Retina images have double the number of pixels that are displayed in an image tag in HTML.

```
<img src="a400x400image.jpg" width="200" height="200">
```

Using 2x Retina images offers an easy design solution for creating sharp images, but what about non-Retina users? Non-Retina users with a slower connection are likely to wait longer for the web page to load. To avoid this, there are a couple of ways to deal with HiDPI images using HTML5:

- **srcset Attribute:** This image tag attribute enables you to specify a list of image sources to use based on the width of the browser and the pixel density of the device.

- **picture Element:** This element allows you to specify multiple sources with the option to fall back to the default non-Retina image.

Scanning, Not Reading, Online Content

People do not read online content, unless it is an EPUB. They skim it, searching for something to catch their eye. It is a very different experience from reading a printed book. People hunt, looking for highlighted keywords, meaningful headings, short paragraphs, and scannable lists. As a designer, you need to design your content to facilitate scanning.

Don't expect people to read long text blocks, unnecessary instructions, or promotional writing on the Web. To assist them in finding the piece of information they're looking for, think about using the following:

- Short sentence fragments for headings
- Small paragraphs of text
- Bulleted or numbered lists
- Limited use of **bold** text for keywords
- Small line length (number of characters per line of text)

Think about how the user will process what they see on a web page:

- **Rough Scan:** At first, the user processes large masses of shapes and colors.

- **Fine-Tune Scan:** The user starts to see separate lines of text and images. They are not reading characters or words yet.

- **Filter Scan:** The user begins to read words and phrases. Headings are quickly scanned to see if the content is what the user wants.

Jakob Nielsen is a usability expert who writes about eye-tracking research at *www.nngroup.com/articles/how-users-read-on-the-web/.*

Elements of Responsive Web Design

Let us explore the principles behind responsive web design. In order to achieve responsive web design, a web page needs to have three key features. Web designer/developer Ethan Marcotte describes these features as follows:

- **Fluid grid layout**
- **Flexible typography and images**
- **CSS3 media queries**

Static versus Fluid Grids

A static, or fixed, grid is built with its content set to a fixed pixel width. Web designers adopted the use of pixel-based grid layouts prior to the popularity of mobile devices. Regardless of the screen size being used to view the site, the static layout will maintain its fixed width. Fluid grids are more carefully designed using proportions rather than fixed pixels.

For a fluid grid design, the goal is to design with flexibility for a variety of screen dimensions. Pixels do not scale according to the width of the browser window. So, a pixel-based web page design won't adapt to the width of the browser. Fluid grid systems use percentages, because they are relative units that adjust to either the height or width of a parent element.

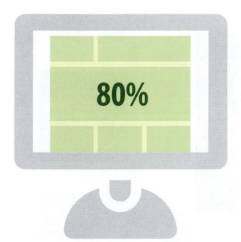

Use percentages for a container's width to accommodate different device screen displays. For example, setting the container's width at 80% will place it comfortably in a desktop's large display, while a width of 98% maximizes the layout for a single column of content on a mobile screen.

Flexible Typography and Images

In CSS, an em unit is equal to the current font size. The default size of text in a browser is 16 pixels. If the font size of the document is 16 points, 1 em is equal to 16 points. Ems are scalable, so 2 em would equal 32 points. The percent unit is similar to the em unit. If the current font size is equal to 100%,16 points equals 100%.

HTML & CSS: Designing and Building Websites by Jon Duckett is a good resource for learning CSS in regard to typography.

px	em	%
16 px	1 em	100%
24 px	1.5 em	150%
32 px	2 em	200%

In addition to typography, images can be set up as flexible elements that move and scale with the fluid grid. This is fairly easy to do using Cascading Style Sheets (CSS). Setting the image's maximum width to 100% forces the image's width to match the width of its container.

An easy solution to creating a flexible image is to assign the CSS rule max-width which scales the image using a percentage relative width value: **img {max-width:100%}**.

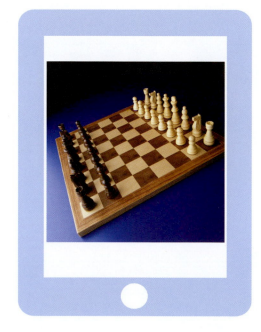

What Are Media Queries?

Responsive design is built around the concept of media queries that target specific devices and their screen widths. Media queries offer designers the flexibility to design content that is flexible and adaptable. They are currently supported across modern browsers. Media queries gather data about the user (what device he/she is on and the screen resolution) and use it to conditionally apply CSS styles to the content.

There are thousands of screen widths available and you cannot design for every one of them. The best approach to starting out with media queries is to group devices with similar screen widths together such as smartphones and tablets. From there, establish what will serve as the default dimensions during the design process. For example:

- **320 px:** Smartphone Portrait
- **480 px:** Smartphone Landscape
- **768 px**: Tablet Portrait
- **960 px:** Tablet Landscape
- **1024 px:** Large Tablet
- **1280 px:** Laptop
- **1440 px:** Widescreen Desktop

A good resource for seeing media queries in action is at *mediaqueri.es.*

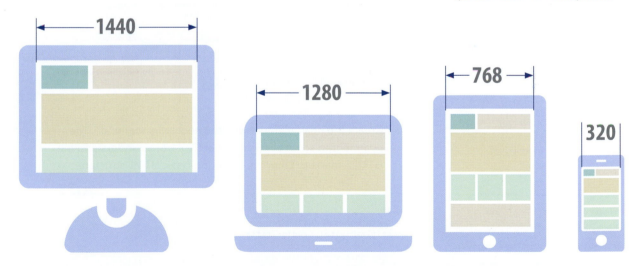

Chapter Exercise:
Building a Responsive Web Layout

Let's take a look at responsive design in action. For the purpose of this exercise, a website will be designed that scales between large and small screens. Media queries will change the user navigation from a horizontal menu to a vertical stacked menu for smaller viewports. The key element is setting up a fluid grid layout.

This exercise uses Adobe Dreamweaver to build a page that contains a content wrapper, a header with navigation, the main content in two columns that will adapt to different device widths, and a footer. To demonstrate the basics of responsive web design, this exercise is broken up into several parts. The first part is to create the actual HTML structure.

PART 1: Creating the Structure

1. Download and uncompress the **Chapter_05.zip** folder to your desktop. The folder contains all the image files needed to complete this exercise. Feel free to substitute your own images.

2. Create a new HTML5 file in Adobe Dreamweaver and save it as **index.html** inside the downloaded folder titled **Chapter_05.**

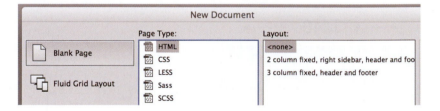

3. Create the head element with the necessary metadata. The commented script allows Internet Explorer to understand the HTML5 markup. Enter the following basic HTML structure:

```
<head>
    <meta charset="utf-8"/>
    <title>Digital Studio</title>
    <!--[if lt IE 9]>
    <script src="//html5shiv.googlecode.com/svn/trunk/html5.js"></script>
    <![endif]-->
</head>
```

Download the exercise file to your hard drive:

www.routledge.com/cw/Jackson

Chapter_05.zip

When working with HTML5, you should include the "HTML5 shiv," which ensures that the CSS will be recognized and correctly applied to the page elements in browsers that are not up to date on the new markup syntax.

4. Add a DIV wrapper and header elements to the body:

```html
<body>

    <div id="wrapper">

        <header>

            <div id="logo">
                <img src="images/logotype.jpg" alt="Digital Studio logo" />
            </div>

            <nav>
                <ul>
                    <li><a href="#" title="About">ABOUT</a></li>
                    <li><a href="#" title="Portfolio">PORTFOLIO</a></li>
                    <li><a href="#" title="Clients">CLIENTS</a></li>
                    <li><a href="#" title="Contact">CONTACT</a></li>
                </ul>
            </nav>

            <div id="banner">
                <img src="images/bannerImage.jpg" alt="New Book advertisement" />
            </div>

        </header>
```

5. Under the header tag, add a new section tag with three articles
   inside the DIV wrapper:

```html
        <section id="mainContent">

            <article id="welcome">
                <h1>Welcome</h1>
                <p>Lorem ipsum dolor sit amet, consectetur adipisicing elit, sed do eiusmod
tempor incididunt ut labore et dolore magna aliqua. Ut enim ad minim veniam, quis nostrud
exercitation ullamco laboris nisi ut aliquip ex ea commodo consequat. Duis aute irure dolor in
reprehenderit in voluptate velit esse cillum dolore eu fugiat nulla pariatur. Excepteur sint
occaecat cupidatat non proident, sunt in culpa qui officia deserunt mollit anim id est laborum.</p>
            </article>

            <article id="mission">
                <h1>Our Mission</h1>
                <p>Consectetur adipisicing elit, sed do eiusmod tempor incididunt ut labore et
dolore magna aliqua. Ut enim ad minim veniam, quis nostrud exercitation ullamco laboris nisi ut
aliquip ex ea commodo consequat.</p>
            </article>

            <article id="vision">
                <h1>Our Vision</h1>
                <p>Ut enim ad minim veniam, quis nostrud exercitation ullamco laboris nisi ut
aliquip ex ea commodo consequat. Duis aute irure dolor in reprehenderit in voluptate. </p>
            </article>

        </section>
```

6. Finally, add an aside tag for news and events and the footer content. Don't forget to close out the open "wrapper" DIV tag:

```
        <aside id="news">
            <h1>News and Events</h1>
            <p>Consectetur adipisicing elit, sed do eiusmod tempor incididunt ut labore et
dolore magna aliqua. Ut enim ad minim veniam, quis nostrud exercitation ullamco laboris nisi ut
aliquip ex ea commodo consequat.</p>
            <img src="images/exhibit.jpg" alt="gallery exhibit" />
        </aside>

        <footer>
            <p>&copy; Digital Studio<p>
        </footer>

    </div>

</body>
```

7. Save your HTML and preview it in a browser.

If you stop and think about it, the concept of a responsive layout is not a new thing. Take a look at the simple HTML file you just built; its content will automatically adapt to fit the width of the browser. The Web is responsive on its own by default. It is just not designed well. That is why we use CSS.

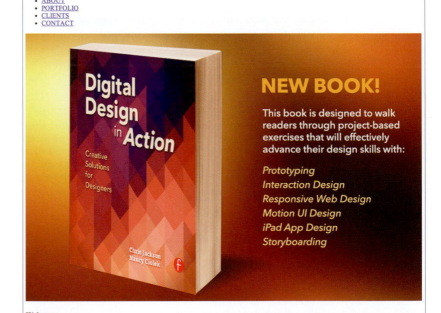

PART 2: Give the Content Some Style

With the HTML structure in place, let's add the CSS styles to the elements. You will be using percentages and ems to create a fluid layout. Also, you will set the image's width to 100% to adapt more easily to the layout.

1. Create a new CSS file in Adobe Dreamweaver and save it into a **new folder** labeled **styles** as **main.css** inside the folder titled **Chapter_05**.

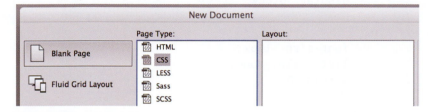

2. Add the CSS link to the <head> element in the **index.html** file.

```
<head>
    <meta charset="utf-8"/>
    <title>Digital Studio</title>
    <link href="styles/main.css" type="text/css" rel="stylesheet">
    <!--[if lt IE 9]>
    <script src="//html5shiv.googlecode.com/svn/trunk/html5.js"></script>
    <![endif]-->
</head>
```

It is always best practice to keep your CSS styles external from the HTML.

3. Go to the new CSS file and add the following rules for the elements. First, you will clear out all the margin and padding default settings that the browser uses. This gives you a clean slate to design with.

```
1  /* Reset Default Broswer Margins and Padding */
2  * {
3      margin: 0;
4      padding: 0;
5  }
6
```

This is a very popular technique as it removes all default margin and padding for every object on the page, regardless of the browser.

4. Continue to define new styles for the HTML elements. Set the default text size, its color, and adjust the unordered list. See the CSS markup on the following page.

This defines the default font, its size, and color for the entire page. It also loads a tiled background image to repeat vertically and horizontally.

The unordered list holds all the navigational hyperlink text. The text is increased to 16 pixels to make it easier to tap on mobile devices.

This defines the look for the navigation. It removes the underline from the hyperlinks and changes the font style to bold instead of roman.

The aside column's text is decreased in size to 90% (0.9 em). The font style is also changed to italic.

```css
 7   /* Define Element Styles */
 8   body {
 9       font-family: Arial, helvetica, sans-serif;
10       font-size: 14px;
11       color: #666666;
12       background-image: url(../images/grid.jpg)
13   }
14   article, aside, footer, header, nav, section {
15       display: block;
16   }
17   ul {
18       font-size: 16px;
19       list-style: none;
20       margin: 0;
21   }
22   ul li {
23       margin: 0;
24       padding: 0;
25   }
26   h1 {
27       font-size: 24px;
28       margin-bottom: 10px;
29       color: #111111;
30   }
31   a {
32       outline: none;
33       border: none;
34       color: #666666;
35       font-weight: bold;
36       text-decoration:none;
37   }
38   a:hover {
39       color: #ffb100;
40   }
41   p {
42       margin: 0 0 10px;
43       line-height: 1.4em;
44       font-size: 1.2em;
45   }
46   img {
47       display: block;
48       margin-bottom: 10px;
49   }
50   aside {
51       font-style: italic;
52       font-size: 0.9em;
53   }
54
```

5. Next, define the fluid grid layout. First, you need to set up the main DIV wrapper that holds all of the HTML elements. By setting its width to 98%, it will sit comfortably on smaller display sizes. The maximum width it can be is 960 pixels for desktop displays.

```
55   /* Stylize the Structure */
56   #wrapper {
57       width: 98%;
58       max-width: 960px;
59       margin: auto;
60       padding: 0 1% 0 1%;
61       background-color: white;
62       overflow: hidden;
63       -moz-box-shadow: 0px 1px 30px #582045;
64       -webkit-box-shadow: 0px 1px 30px #582045;
65       box-shadow: 0px 1px 30px #582045;
66   }
67   #mainContent {
68       width: 55%;
69       margin-right: 5%;
70       float: left;
71   }
72   #news {
73       width: 40%;
74       float: right;
75   }
76   #news img {
77       width: 100%;
78       margin-top: 3%;
79       margin-bottom: 30px;
80   }
81   #logo {
82       height: 70px;
83       width: 50%;
84       float: left;
85       display: block;
86       margin-top: 15px;
87       margin-bottom: 5px;
88   }
89   header nav {
90       float: right;
91       margin-top: 57px;
92   }
93   header nav li {
94       display: inline;
95       margin-left: 15px;
96   }
```

To make sure that the box shadow will display the same on all browsers, use the correct browser support:

moz = Firefox

webkit = Chrome, Safari, and Opera

CSS floats push an element to the left or right, allowing other elements to wrap around it. For this two-column layout, the left column's width equals 55% and the right column's width equals 40%. With a 5% margin added in between the two columns, the total size equals 100%.

The user navigation is aligned to the right edge of the layout using a float.

Setting the image's width to 100% will allow it to scale within its container.

You do not want the footer to float next to the content. The clear property stops the element from floating next to the two columns.

```css
 97  #banner {
 98      float: left;
 99      margin-bottom: 15px;
100      width: 100%;
101  }
102  #banner img {
103      width: 100%;
104  }
105  article {
106      margin-bottom: 20px;
107  }
108  footer {
109      clear:both;
110      width: 100%;
111      height: 40px;
112      background-color: black;
113      border-radius: 20px 20px 0px 0px;
114      text-align:center;
115      padding-top: 20px;
116  }
117  footer p {
118      color: white;
119  }
120
```

6. Save your HTML and CSS. Preview the HTML in a browser. Click and drag the browser window to scale it to different sizes. Notice how the content scales with it.

PART 3: Make It Responsive

The design is getting there, but the navigation, in its current state, could be hard to tap on when displayed on a mobile device. It also does not align as well as it could in the smaller browser width. By using media queries, you can design it to allow the user to access it more easily.

1. Go to the new CSS file and add the following media queries after the CSS rules you just created:

```
121   /*  Set Media Queries */
122   @media screen and (max-width: 810px) {
123
124   #wrapper {
125       padding: 0 2% 0 2%;
126   }
127   #logo {
128       width: 100%;
129       margin-bottom: 0px;
130   }
131   #logo img {
132       display: block;
133       margin: 0 auto;
134   }
135   header nav, #mainContent, #news {
136       float: left;
137       clear: left;
138       margin: 0 0 10px;
139       width: 100%;
140   }
141   header nav li {
142       margin: 0;
143       background: #ffd2f4;
144       display: block;
145       margin-bottom: 5px;
146   }
147   header nav a {
148       display: block;
149       padding: 10px 0px 5px 0px;
150       text-align: center;
151       vertical-align: middle;
152   }
153   a:hover {
154       color: #666666;
155   }
156
157   }
158
```

For screens that are smaller than 810 pixels …

The logo element scales down with the smaller display width. Its alignment is also centered on the screen.

At the smaller size, the two columns are switched to one column of content.

The navigation menu is converted to a block menu to allow the user to interact with it more easily on smaller displays.

```
159    @media screen and (max-width: 400px) {
160
161    #wrapper {
162        padding: 0 4% 0 4%;
163    }
164    #logo img {
165        width: 100%;
166    }
167    #banner {
168        display: none;
169    }
170    article {
171        margin-bottom: 10px;
172    }
173    article h1, aside h1 {
174        text-align: center;
175    }
176
177    }
```

This second media query removes the banner image and just displays the text in one column.

2. Save your CSS file. Go to the HTML file and add the following in the <head> element. This will scale the web page correctly for smaller smartphone displays.

```
<head>
    <meta charset="utf-8"/>
    <meta name="viewport" content="width=device-width, initial-scale=1.0" />
    <title>Digital Studio</title>
    <link href="styles/main.css" type="text/css" rel="stylesheet">
    <!--[if lt IE 9]>
    <script src="//html5shiv.googlecode.com/svn/trunk/html5.js"></script>
    <![endif]-->
</head>
```

The width property controls the size of the viewport. It can be set to a specific device-width value, which is the width of the screen in pixels at a scale of 100%. The initial-scale property is set to 1, or 100%, to scale correctly on all displays.

3. Save your HTML and preview it in a browser. Click and drag the browser window to scale it to different sizes. Congratulations! You have made a responsive web layout.

DIGITALSTUDIO

ABOUT PORTFOLIO CLIENTS CONTACT

NEW BOOK!

This book is designed to walk readers through project-based exercises that will effectively advance their design skills with:

Prototyping
Interaction Design
Responsive Web Design
Motion UI Design
iPad App Design
Storyboarding

Welcome

Lorem ipsum dolor sit amet, consectetur adipisicing elit, sed do eiusmod tempor incididunt ut labore et dolore magna aliqua. Ut enim ad minim veniam, quis nostrud exercitation ullamco laboris nisi ut aliquip ex ea commodo consequat. Duis aute irure dolor in reprehenderit in voluptate velit esse cillum dolore eu fugiat nulla pariatur. Excepteur sint occaecat cupidatat non proident, sunt in culpa qui officia deserunt mollit anim id est laborum.

Our Mission

Consectetur adipisicing elit, sed do eiusmod tempor incididunt ut

News and Events

Consectetur adipisicing elit, sed do eiusmod tempor incididunt ut labore et dolore magna aliqua. Ut enim ad minim veniam, quis nostrud exercitation ullamco laboris nisi ut aliquip ex ea commodo consequat.

GALLERY EXHIBITION NYC

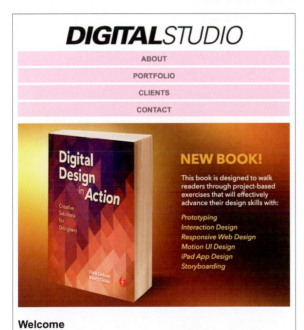

DIGITALSTUDIO

ABOUT

PORTFOLIO

CLIENTS

CONTACT

NEW BOOK!

This book is designed to walk readers through project-based exercises that will effectively advance their design skills with:

Prototyping
Interaction Design
Responsive Web Design
Motion UI Design
iPad App Design
Storyboarding

Welcome

Lorem ipsum dolor sit amet, consectetur adipisicing elit, sed do eiusmod tempor incididunt ut labore et dolore magna aliqua. Ut enim ad minim veniam, quis nostrud exercitation ullamco laboris nisi ut aliquip ex ea commodo consequat. Duis aute irure dolor in reprehenderit in voluptate velit esse cillum dolore eu fugiat nulla pariatur. Excepteur sint occaecat cupidatat non proident, sunt in culpa qui officia deserunt mollit anim id est laborum.

DIGITALSTUDIO

ABOUT

PORTFOLIO

CLIENTS

CONTACT

Welcome

Lorem ipsum dolor sit amet, consectetur adipisicing elit, sed do eiusmod tempor incididunt ut labore et dolore magna aliqua. Ut enim ad minim veniam, quis nostrud exercitation ullamco laboris nisi ut aliquip ex ea commodo consequat. Duis aute irure dolor in reprehenderit in voluptate velit esse cillum dolore eu fugiat nulla pariatur. Excepteur sint occaecat cupidatat non proident, sunt in culpa qui officia deserunt mollit anim id est laborum.

Our Mission

Consectetur adipisicing elit, sed do eiusmod tempor incididunt ut labore et dolore magna aliqua. Ut enim ad minim veniam, quis nostrud exercitation ullamco laboris nisi ut aliquip ex ea commodo consequat.

Our Vision

Ut enim ad minim veniam, quis nostrud exercitation ullamco laboris nisi ut aliquip ex ea commodo consequat. Duis aute irure dolor in reprehenderit in voluptate.

News and Events

Consectetur adipisicing elit, sed do eiusmod tempor incididunt ut labore et dolore magna aliqua. Ut enim ad minim veniam, quis nostrud exercitation ullamco laboris nisi ut aliquip ex ea commodo consequat.

GALLERY EXHIBITION NYC August 17th

© Digital Studio

Summary

Responsive web design is about adapting layouts to different screen sizes. As designers we must accept that screen sizes will always be changing and embrace the challenge to design flexible layouts that adapt to any screen size, today and in the future.

Key principles that designer should follow are:

- Do not use pixels for fixed heights.
- Do not create the need for horizontal scroll bars.
- Design your images to look consistent at different sizes.
- Design your content to wrap.

This completes this chapter. You should now be able to:

- Apply design principles to screen layouts for mobile devices.
- Discuss mobile design patterns and best practices.
- Design an HTML layout that changes based on the size and capabilities of the device.
- Optimize content that responds to the needs of the users and the devices they are using.

The next chapter focuses on digital design in motion.

6

Integrating Motion in Digital Design

Animation is an illusion. It is a representation of movement or change in time. A web designer's role needs to go beyond creating a series of linked online documents. Learning animation skills and principles help bring content and graphical user interfaces to life. Animation is not a new concept, but designers are now, more than ever, incorporating motion as an integral component in online communication.

This chapter explores how to translate motion principles into digital design projects to enhance the overall user experience. At the completion of this chapter, you will be able to:

- Describe several motion principles and how they can translate to digital design.
- Discuss the benefits of incorporating motion into a UI design.
- Apply CSS transitions and animation to web content.
- Describe simulating depth using parallax movement.
- Build a web page that incorporates parallax scrolling.

The Illusion of Movement

In film, a frame is a single still image. The illusion of movement occurs when frames are shown in rapid succession. This is often referred to as **persistence of vision**. This phenomenon takes place in the eye where a frame's afterimage is thought to persist for approximately one 1/25th of a second on the retina. This afterimage is overlapped by the next frame's image and we interpret it as continuous movement.

Frame Rates Impact Human Perception of Motion

Frame rate is the speed at which the frames are played back to the viewer. The default frame rate for a theatrical film is 24 frames per second (fps). The smoothness of the movement is affected by its frame rate. Some common frames-per-second settings used today include:

- **12 fps:** Minimum speed required for the illusion of movement
- **24 fps:** Standard frame rate for film
- **30 fps:** Standard frame rate for NTSC video
- **60 fps:** Threshold above which most people will not perceive smoother images

Persistence of vision is an optical illusion of movement.

Motion Principles

HTML is the underlying structure that allows designers to create sites that communicate information and tell stories. Similar to using hierarchy that guides users through content, motion can facilitate the journey by helping users understand relationships, orientation, and cause and effect.

Animation focuses on time, and provides an illusion of realistic movement that occurs in our world such as gravity, reaction, squash and stretch. In the 1930s, Walt Disney published a set of twelve animation principles that provided established guidelines for traditional animators. Some of these principles translate well in creating UI motion design.

For more information on animation and the twelve principles, read **The Illusion of Life: Disney Animation** by Frank Thomas and Ollie Johnston.

Solid Drawing

This principle focuses on the appearance of an object and its potential for movement. It provides a tangible link to three-dimensional real things that can react to pushing, spinning, or dragging. Solidity helps separate the interactive UI elements from the static content.

Squash and Stretch

This movement shows an object's mass and flexibility as it moves. An important concept to remember is that a object's volume does not change when it is squashed or stretched. In UI motion design, squash and stretch is used to provide feedback when a button is clicked, tapped, or hovered over.

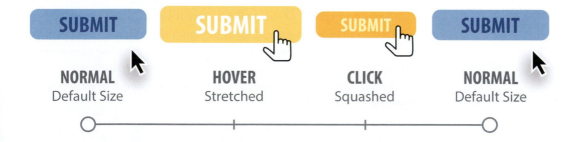

NORMAL	HOVER	CLICK	NORMAL
Default Size	Stretched	Squashed	Default Size

Anticipation

This action alerts the user to a movement that is about to occur. Anticipation is a subtle contrary movement just before the main move, such as a small backward motion occurring before an object moves forward. It provides a clue to the movement that follows, and without it the movement can appear unexpected and even jarring to the user. In UI motion design, content panels can shrink or expand prior to their main action of revealing or hiding the information.

INTERACTION
Panel Tapped

ANTICIPATION
Panel Shrinks

ANIMATION
Panel Expands

Follow-through and Overlapping Action

Follow-through shows an object bounce or wiggle at the end of its motion, as if attached to a spring. Overlapping action observes that parts of an object do not all come to a standstill at the same time. These parts move at different speeds and require extra time to catch up to the main movement. In UI motion design, both principles work together to help indicate relationships, such as how a collection of apps, menu items, or thumbnail images are all interrelated.

Arcs

This movement mimics the slight circular path that objects tend to move along in our world. This provides consistent and predictable motion to UI elements. A common example is a spinning carousel gallery where objects are connected to a circular track.

Offsetting the animation time for the menu items communicates the chronological order for completion at the same time that it displays how the tasks are interrelated.

Slow-In and Slow-Out

Objects in our world gradually accelerate into motion or gradually decelerate out of motion. Think about when a driver puts his foot on the gas pedal. The car does not instantly move at the speed limit; it gradually accelerates over time as it travels down the road. In UI motion design, this is achieved through **easing** functions in CSS and JavaScript.

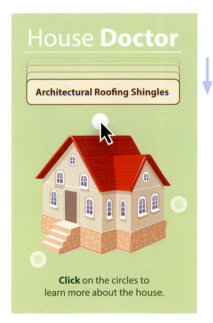

The principle of slow-in and slow-out is applied to UI drop-down panels (left image) and scrolling lists (right image). Robert Penner defined easing equations in code. His library of easing functions are widely used today.

Benefits of Motion

Translating the motion principles into a static, two-dimensional digital document can help users understand what they're looking at. It can keep the user aware of their tasks at hand and where they are. Applying motion principles to your project provides many benefits, such as:

- **Guidance:** Motion provides a natural flow at a distinct pace for the user to follow

- **Focus:** Motion draws attention to objects and actions

- **Orientation:** Motion provides a sense of bearing for the user

- **Engagement:** Motion can add additional appeal and sense of delight to the content

Movement can help users understand where they have come from as they navigate to a new page. A horizontal slide from one screen to another facilitates guidance and orientation.

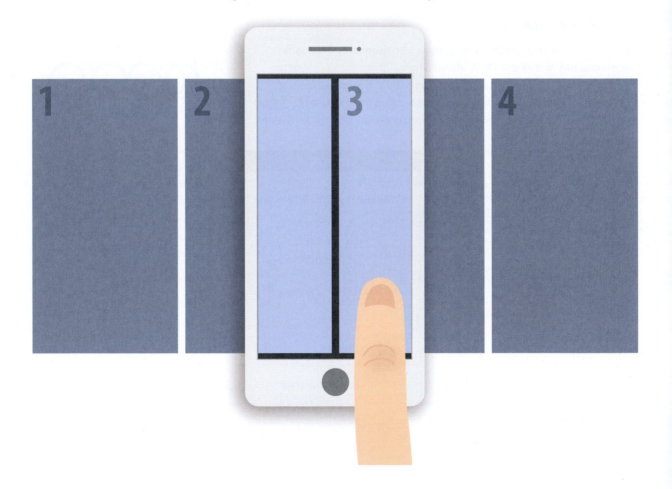

User experience design focuses on how users feel as they interact with the content. Motion adds another dimension of realism to the elements on the screen. This provides users with the feeling of connectivity and control as they see how their actions physically change the UI and its content. By proper application, motion can indicate user control through:

- **Cause and effect**: When two events occur one right after the other, our brains interpret that the two events are related and that the first caused the second. When users click on a submit button and an online form disappears, they determine that they caused the action.

- **Feedback**: This indicates to a user that their actions triggered a response. UI elements should grow, shrink, expand, rotate, or collapse to communicate change.

- **Progression**: Motion can show the user's journey through a linear sequence. It can also depict what the system is currently doing such as with an animated loading bar or spinning hourglass.

- **Relationships:** Motion can depict where things are hierarchically and spatially in relation to one another. Movement can enhance the user's perception of depth.

- **Transition**: This motion indicates changes in the content, location, or time. This helps orient the user to where they are and how they are moving through the content.

Motion makes buttons and other UI elements feel responsive and alive to the user. Keep the animation subtle. It is easy to overwhelm the user with complex animation moving all over the screen. The goal is to focus the user's attention. Where do you want your user to look?

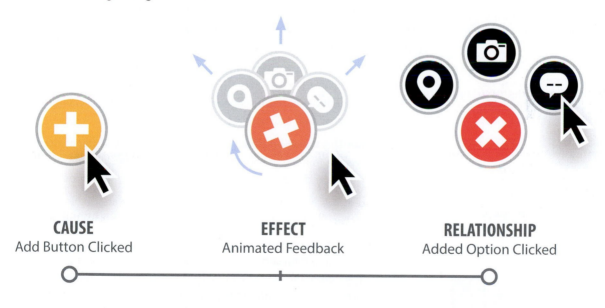

CAUSE
Add Button Clicked

EFFECT
Animated Feedback

RELATIONSHIP
Added Option Clicked

A good article on easing can be found at *medium.com/@sureshvselvaraj/animation-principles-in-ui-design-understanding-easing-bea05243fe3*.

Transitions help preserve continuity in the content.

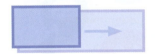

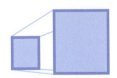

Too Much Motion?

Even though there are a lot of benefits to motion design, be careful not to overdo it. Just as motion can focus the user's attention, it can be disruptive to the overall user experience if misused. When adding motion to your projects, follow these best practices:

- **Less is more:** Too much animation creates visual noise and the user will lose focus on the content. Be subtle with the motion. Only use it when needed to draw the user's attention.

- **Be complimentary:** Make sure the motion serves a purpose to highlight the content, show progression, or provide feedback to the user's actions.

- **Don't take forever:** Animation is all about timing. The user should not have to sit through a long animation or screen transition. The timing required needs to effectively show a change without interfering with the system's perceived responsiveness.

Movement and Meaning

Creating transitions for interface elements is part of designing websites and mobile apps today. Applying the smallest movement can have a deep impact on the user's experience. In film, the goal in editing a scene is that you want the audience to presume that time and space have been uninterrupted. So how do you transition from one scene to the next and still preserve continuity?

- **Fade:** This is a common transition used in early filmmaking at the start and end of every sequence. A fade increases or decreases the overall value of the scene into one color. Fades indicate the passage of time or inactivity.

- **Wipe:** This transition clearly marks the change. One scene wipes across the frame and replaces the previous scene. Wipes can move in any direction and open from one side to the other.

- **Zoom:** This is an optical effect that magnifies the image. Scaling objects communicates hierarchy and provides focus for the user.

- **Clean Entrances and Exits:** If an object exits the frame, hold the empty frame for a second or two. Then show the second screen empty before the object enters the frame. By not seeing the object on screen for a second or two, the user will accept that it had time to travel to the different location in the following screen.

Animating with CSS

How does a designer apply motion principles to a website? In addition to changing HTML properties using Cascading Style Sheets (CSS), transitions and transforms are also available. They allow designers to use CSS, with no JavaScript coding, to animate certain properties of elements on a web page.

CSS Transition Properties

If you change the color of an element from red to blue it will change instantly. With CSS transitions enabled, the change can now occur at a set time interval with easing functions applied. CSS transitions are controlled using the shorthand **transition** property. The individual components of the transition are controlled with the following sub-properties:

- **transition-property**: Specifies the name or names of the CSS properties that will be affected by the transition. Properties such as color, opacity, background color, letter spacing can be animated during transitions.

- **transition-duration**: Specifies how long the transitions will occur. This can be specified as a single duration that applies to all the properties during the transition, or multiple values that allow each property to transition over a different period of time.

- **transition-timing-function**: Specifies a transition's change in speed over its duration. Easing functions are similar to the animation principle of slow-in and slow-out and make the transition feel more natural, mirroring the way objects move in real life. There are several types of eases:

  ◊ **linear:** The transition occurs at the same speed from start to finish

  ◊ **ease:** The transition begins with a slow start, then gets faster, then ends slowly

  ◊ **ease-in:** The transition begins with a slow start

  ◊ **ease-out:** The transition finishes with a slow end

  ◊ **ease-in-out:** The transition begins with a slow start and finishes with a slow end

- **transition-delay**: Specifies how long to wait between the time a property is changed and when the transition actually begins.

A good resource for CSS transitions and transforms can be found at *css3.bradshawenterprises.com.*

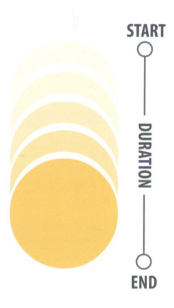

START

DURATION

END

CSS Transforms

Transitions change CSS properties over a specified time. Transforms actually manipulate HTML objects, such as divs and images. CSS can be used to transform these elements in both two- and three-dimensional space. All transforms follow the same basic syntax:

- The shorthand **transform** property
- The function name with any parameters in parentheses. Parameters are often numerical and help the transform complete its function. There are four basic transform functions:

    ◊ **Translate**: This transform moves objects around the screen. Positive numbers move the target element right and down based on pixels. You can also use negative values to move elements up and left.

    ◊ **Scale:** This transform takes two parameters, (width) X and (height) Y, where 1 equals the size as the original, .5 is half the size, and 2 is twice the scale.

    ◊ **Rotate:** This transform rotates an element clockwise at a given degree. Negative values rotate the element counterclockwise.

    ◊ **Skew:** This transform turns the element in a given angle, depending on the parameters given for the horizontal (X-axis) and the vertical (Y-axis) lines.

Another resource for CSS transitions and transforms can be found at *www.w3schools.com/css/css3_animations.asp*.

HTML

```
<div id="box"> </div>
```

CSS

```
div {
    width: 300px;
    height: 300px;
    background-color: orange;
    border: 1px solid black;
}

div#box {
    -ms-transform: rotate(45deg);  /* IE 9 */
    -webkit-transform: rotate(45deg); /* Safari */
    transform: rotate(45deg); /* Standard syntax */
}
```

BROWSER

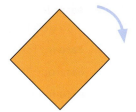

CSS Animation

You can also create a CSS animation sequence using the animation property and its sub-properties. You can configure the timing and duration of the animation using the **@keyframes** rule. A **keyframe** defines how the animated element should render at a given time during the animation sequence. The rule uses a percentage to keep track of the time during the animation sequence. Zero percent (0%) indicates the start of the animation sequence, while 100% indicates the completion of the animation.

For more information on CSS animation, read *Animation in HTML, CSS, and JavaScript* by Kirupa Chinnnathambi.

- The animation sub-properties include:
  - ◊ **animation-name:** This specifies the name of the @keyframes rule that performs the animation's keyframes.
  - ◊ **animation-duration:** This sets the length of time that an animation will take to complete.
  - ◊ **animation-delay:** This specifies the delay between the time the element is loaded and the start of the animation.
  - ◊ **animation-iteration-count:** This defines the number of times the animation should repeat.
  - ◊ **animation-play-state:** This allows you to pause and resume the animation.
- The shorthand **@keyframes** rule with the **animation-name** group the animation sequence.

HTML

<div id="box"> </div>

CSS

```
div#box {
    width: 100px;
    height: 100px;
    background-color: red;
    position: relative;
    animation-name: moveBox;
    animation-duration: 4s;
}

@keyframes moveBox {
    0%  { background-color:red; left:0px; top:0px; }
    25% { background-color:yellow; left:400px; top:0px; }
    50% { background-color:blue; left:400px; top:400px; }
    75% { background-color:green; left:0px; top:400px; }
    100% { background-color:red; left:0px; top:0px; }
}
```

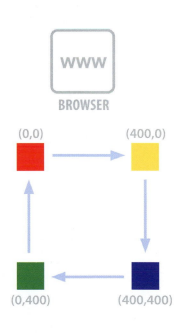

BROWSER

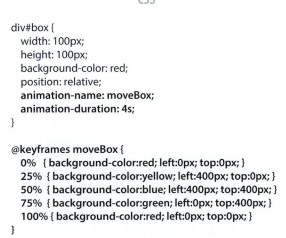

Simulating Depth with Motion

Visual depth cues, such as relative size, shadows, and perspective, add dimension to a still image. As the viewer, we can determine what is in the foreground, middle ground, and background. As a static image, the scene has gone as far as it can in simulating a three-dimensional world. Movement further enhances our perception of depth.

Parallax scrolling is an animation technique where background images move by the camera slower than foreground images. This creates an illusion of depth in a 2D scene.

Parallax scrolling is a popular animation technique used in web design today. It simulates three-dimensional motion on a page using a scroll effect. So, what is parallax scrolling? Remember the last time you were riding in a car looking out at the passing landscape. The car was moving at a consistent speed, but different parts of the landscape appeared to be moving at different speeds. Objects farthest away, such as rolling hills, appear smaller and move slower when compared to objects in the foreground that race past the car. How does this happen?

The illusion is caused by two factors. One is your viewing position or vantage point, and the other is the relative distance the objects are from you. Imagine you are in a helicopter looking straight down on three people crossing a street. Each person moves the same distance in the same amount of time. From your viewpoint above, you witness a consistent speed and distance traveled.

Now imagine yourself sitting in a car watching the same three people cross the street. The speed and distance traveled appear to differ for each person. Why? When we change our vantage point, we see more of the space surrounding each person. Each person moves relative to the space they occupy. Objects closer to us will appear to travel farther and move more quickly than objects farther away.

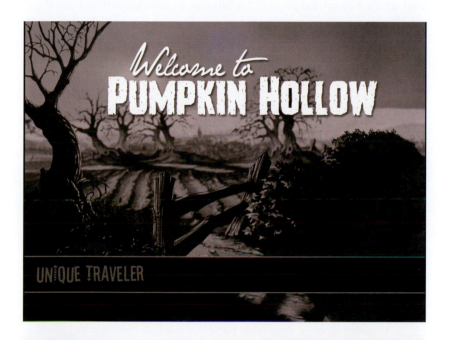

In the Pumpkin Hollow example (left), parallax scrolling allows the different elements (background, trees, fence, and logotype) on a page to move in at different speeds with the scroll of the mouse. This creates the illusion of depth.

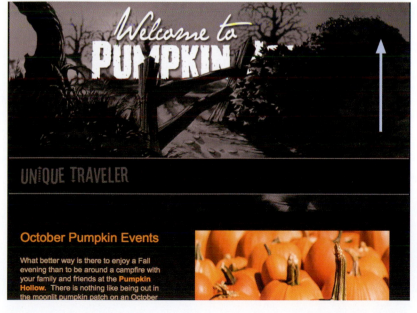

Parallax scrolling on a web page relies on HTML5, CSS, and JavaScript. The actual parallax scrolling movement comes from JavaScript coding. Adobe Muse can apply parallax scrolling to your pages without you having to write a single line of code.

Chapter Exercise:
Scrolling in Adobe Muse

Let's take a look at parallax scrolling in action. **Scroll effects** provide an illusion of depth. For example, a web page layout may include elements in a foreground layer that move faster than other elements when the user scrolls through the page in the browser. In addition to the physical scrolling, scroll effects can also animate to any anchor tag on the page. When the user clicks on a link on a long, vertical page, it causes a scroll to the designated anchor tag, to make different sections appear to fly in, fade in, or animate into place.

In Adobe Muse, there is a panel devoted to scroll effects. To set up the scroll effects, there are three components needed:

- **Initial Motion:** This determines the movement of the element prior to the browser moving past the Key Position when scrolled. The initial motion is set at 1 times (the same speed as) the rate of scrolling. A setting of 0.5x will move at half the speed of the page scroll. A setting of 2x moves the element twice as fast as the page scroll.

- **Key Position:** This is a pixel value on the web page that triggers the scroll effect. For example, the top of the web page begins at 0 and then the number of pixels increases the farther a user scrolls down. As the user scrolls, that specific point will reach the top of a browser window. When that happens, the scroll effect is triggered and performs its movement.

- **Final Motion:** This determines the movement of the object once the browser moves past the Key Position when scrolled. It works similar to the Initial Motion settings.

Download the exercise file to your hard drive:

www.routledge.com/cw/Jackson

Chapter_06.zip

PART 1: Scrolling a Background Fill

1. Download and decompress the **Chapter_06.zip** folder to your desktop. The folder contains all the image files needed to complete this exercise. A completed version of this exercise has also been included for you for reference, if needed.

2. Open the **Parallax START.muse** file inside the folder. The default Plan mode in Adobe Muse is the site map that displays a structured list of the pages that exist in a website's hierarchy. The file contains one web page needed to complete this exercise.

3. Double-click on the **Home** page thumbnail. This opens the page in the Design mode in Adobe Muse. This web page is for a fictitious travel agency. The header artwork is currently missing from the site.

4. Adobe Muse provides a Layers panel that allows you to structure your page elements. Multiple layers help separate specific areas or content on a page without you accidentally changing other content. For this exercise, you will use the stacked layers to create the parallax scroll effect. Open the **Layers** panel and select the **Clouds** layer.

The Site Map in Adobe Muse makes it easy for you to create and rearrange web pages in any order you prefer.

5. Select the **Rectangle** tool. Draw a rectangle that spans the top header of the page; make sure the width of the box is at 100% and its height is 400 pixels. This box element will hold the clouds artwork as a background fill. The fill will move as the page scrolls, based on the directions and speeds you set in the Scroll section of the Fill menu. Let's see how it works.

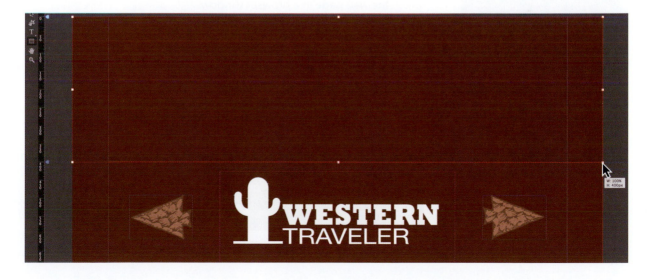

6. Click on the **Fill** menu and select **Add image** next to the Image section. In the Import dialog box, browse to select the file in the **images** folder named **clouds.jpg** and then click **Open**.

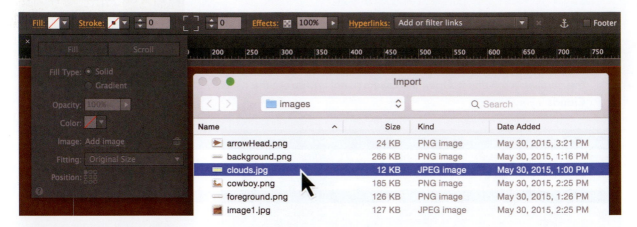

7. Set the Fitting menu to **Tile Horizontally** and click the **center square** in the Position section to center the image on the page.

8. Click on the **Scroll** button next to Fill. Enable the **Motion check box** to activate the scrolling parameters.

9. For the initial vertical direction, set the **up** arrow speed to **1**.

10. For the initial horizontal direction, enter **0.1** for the **left** arrow.

11. Set the **Key Position** parameter to **zero (0) pixels**. This will activate the motion immediately when the user scrolls down the web page in a browser window.

12. For the final vertical motion, set the **up** arrow speed to **1**.

13. For the final horizontal motion, enter **0.1** for the **left** arrow.

14. The last thing you need to do is lock this box in place so that it does not scroll off the top of the browser window. To do this, select the **top center square** in the Pin section.

15. Choose **File > Preview Page in Browser**. Scroll down the page and notice that clouds slowly move to the left.

16. Return to Adobe Muse. Copy the box that holds the clouds image. Open the **Layers** panel and select the **Background** layer.

17. Choose **Edit > Paste in Place**. You will use this copy to replace the artwork with another image and change its motion speed.

18. Click on the **Fill** menu and select **clouds.jpg** next to the Image section. In the Import dialog box, browse to select the file in the **images** folder named **background.png** and then click **Open**.

19. Click on the **Scroll** button next to Fill. All you need to do is slightly increase the horizontal motion to achieve the parallax scroll effect. Increase the initial horizontal direction to **0.5** for the **left** arrow. Increase the final horizontal motion to **0.5** for the **left** arrow.

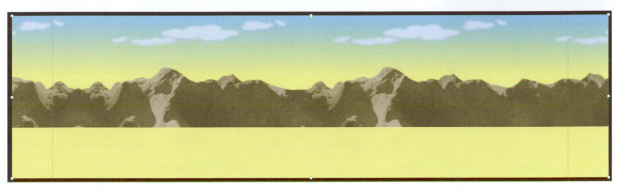

20. Open the **Layers** panel and select the **Middleground** layer.

21. Choose **Edit > Paste in Place**. You will use this new copy to replace the artwork with another image and change its motion speed.

22. Click on the **Fill** menu and select **clouds.jpg** next to the Image section. In the Import dialog box, browse to select the file in the **images** folder named **middleground.png** and then click **Open**.

23. Set the Fitting menu to **Tile Horizontally** and click the **bottom center square** in the Position section to lower the image in the box.

24. Click on the **Scroll** button next to Fill. Increase the initial horizontal direction to **1** for the **left** arrow. Increase the final horizontal motion to **1** for the **left** arrow.

Once the first scrolling layer has been set up to animate, it is easier to copy that container and paste it onto other layers. Then simply replace the artwork and change the motion speeds.

25. Open the **Layers** panel and select the **Foreground** layer.

26. Choose **Edit > Paste in Place**. You will use this new copy to replace the artwork with another image and change its motion speed.

27. Click on the **Fill** menu and select **clouds.jpg** next to the Image section. In the Import dialog box, browse to select the file in the **images** folder named **foreground.png** and then click **Open**.

28. Set the Fitting menu to **Tile Horizontally** and click the **bottom center square** in the Position section to lower the image in the box.

29. Click on the **Scroll** button next to Fill. Increase the initial horizontal direction to **2** for the **left** arrow. Increase the final horizontal motion to **2** for the **left** arrow.

30. Choose **File > Preview Page in Browser**. Scroll down the page to see the completed parallax scroll effect.

For more information on Adobe Muse, read *Creative Web Design with Adobe Muse* by David Asch.

PART 2: Using the Scroll Effects Panel

The scroll effect can also animate individual elements as the user scrolls down the page. Graphics and text frames are controlled using the Scroll Effects panel. Let's explore how to use it:

1. Return to Adobe Muse. Select the Western Traveler logo art.

2. Open the **Motion** tab of the Scroll Effects panel and enable the Motion check box.

3. For the **Initial Motion** section, set the logo to move down at the same speed of scrolling (**1x**).

4. Set the **Key Position** for the logo to **350 pixels**. As the web page reaches this key position for the logo, the logo is positioned at its final location in the background header image.

5. Finally, set the **Final Motion** settings to **0** for both directions. This causes the logo to remain in place, as if it were pinned.

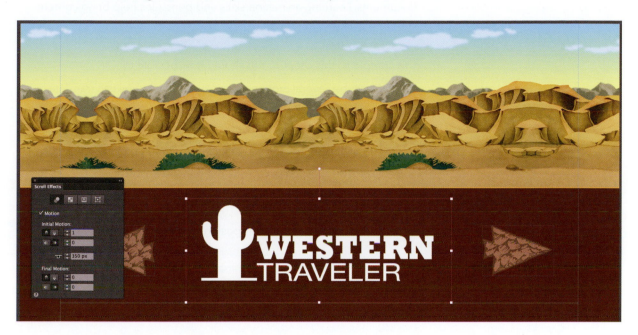

6. Choose **File > Preview Page in Browser**. Scroll down the page to see the animated logo move into position.

The top of the web page begins at 0 and then the number increases as you scroll down the page.

7. Experiment with moving the other elements on the page. Open the **Parallax_DONE.muse** file inside the **Chapter_06** folder. Choose **File > Preview Page in Browser**. Scroll down the page to see examples of what you can do with the arrowheads and the cowboy.

Summary

This chapter explored how to translate motion principles into digital design projects to enhance the overall user experience. Animation is an illusion. It is a representation of movement or change in time. A web designer's role needs to go beyond creating a series of linked online documents. Learning animation skills and principles help bring content and graphical user interfaces to life.

This completes this chapter. You should now be able to:

- Describe several motion principles and how they can translate to digital design.
- Discuss the benefits of incorporating motion into a UI design.
- Apply CSS transitions and animation to web content.
- Describe simulating depth using parallax movement.
- Incorporate parallax scrolling in a web page.

The next chapter focuses on composing interactive forms.

7

Composing Interactive Forms

Forms are often a utilitarian necessity. With the onset of digital forms, tech-savvy audiences, and branding identity, forms have become more sophisticated in their visual and interactive components. Forms should be clear, concise, and easy to use. Graphic design can make a form more effective. Information design, a subset of graphic design, can make a form more effective. It is an important aspect for developing a form for web or print use.

This chapter explores how to integrate principles of design and interaction into digital form design. Upon the completion of this chapter, you will be able to:

- Apply design principles for effective form design
- Integrate grids, typography, and interaction elements
- Understand key elements of form content
- Design an interactive fillable PDF form

Form Design

Print continues to have a significant place in the information landscape, but it's sharing that space with an ever-increasing number of platforms (the Web, mobile phones, tablets, e-readers, etc.). As a result, creative professionals must adapt to a dramatic shift in the preferences and expectations of their audiences. Some stories are better told with video than with lengthy text explanations, and the fixed nature of a print page can limit the use of images to a mere few, while an interactive document can include a slide show in which many photos share the same space.

Forms are used to accomplish a variety of tasks, including gathering information. Forms are a key element of e-commerce, social interactions, and productivity-based applications. Applying visual and organizational principles to form design will help make it more effective and friendly for both the user (filling out the form) and the recipient (receives the data from the filled out form). Basically, people do not like filling out forms. Poorly designed forms can be overwhelming and create confusion for the user. The user needs to be able to accomplish the task with the least amount of annoyance. The quality of design can serve as an indicator of credibility. Forms need to be kept simple, easy, and quick to use.

User perception of forms:

- Long and complicated
- Purpose and/or directions are not always clear
- Forced to answer questions, even if the questions seem irrelevant
- Inaccurate labeling of text fields
- Control taken away from the user
- Errors indicated but not clearly identified
- A negative experience can cause the user to just give up, or even leave the website or app.

Examples of form usage under three main categories:

Social Interaction Forms

- Registration
- Account creation
- Profile

Productivity Forms

- Job application
- Voter registration
- Tax reporting

E-Commerce Forms

- Ordering
- Credit application
- Reservations

Owner/recipient problems with forms:

- Multiple requests for the same information
- Collection of useless information
- Form response does not achieve or is not applicable to a set goal
- Information collected is too vague
- The purpose of the form is not adding value
  to the user's experience.

Formulate sound design decisions to make form completion for the user easy, intuitive, and painless.

Form Content Component

- Purpose
- Content flow
- Hierarchy
- Messaging
- Tone
- Language
- Instruction
- Response
- Feedback

Audience-Related Components

- Identification
- Direction
- Visual cues
- Consistency
- Content flow and organization
- Clarity
- Simplicity
- Feedback

Overall Design Considerations

- Keep the process simple
- Provide clear directions and help
- Request only essential information
- Organize the content
- Utilize the contextual relationship of the form contents
- Only use visual elements if they support the content
- Avoid both visual and verbal clutter
- Set a tone with the language and avoid negative wording
- Consider international users
- Keep buttons and fields separate
- Use support text and links to assist the user

Visual Design Considerations

- **Grid** – visual organization, visual consistency, alignment
- **Hierarchy and sequence** – primary, secondary, and tertiary information levels, order of overall content sequence, flow
- **Typography** – legibility and readability, alignment, contrast, weight, size, scale
- **Imagery and graphic elements** – visual organization, direction, supportive vs. decorative, explanatory, iconography, branding
- **Color** – content organization, grouping of content, contrast, theme, feedback, direction

Icons can be used to indicate specific functions.

Form Design Principles in Action

All type is not created equal.

All type is not created equal.

All type is not created equal.

All type is not created equal.

All type is not created equal.

Type size comparison

Type size and weight can create hierarchy, contrast, and impact.

All type is not created equal.

All type is not created equal.

All type is not created equal.

All type is not created equal.

All type is not created equal.

Type weight comparison

Grids are an important organizational element when designing forms.

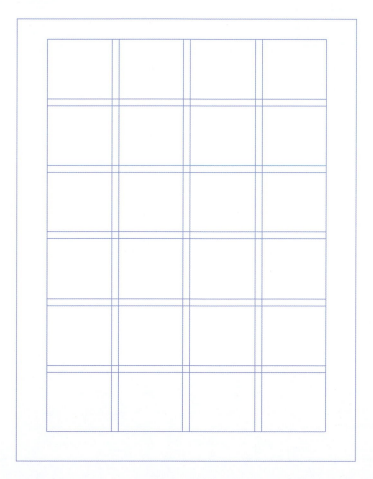

Form Design Principles in Action

The following is an example of a poorly designed form; a well-designed form appears on the right. A generic version of a university form – compiled from various examples – is used to demonstrate hierarchy, organization of content, language, branding, and usability.

Avoid centered type. Harder to read and interrupts the flow of content.
No brand identity of the organization is evident.

No clear hierachy of information. Visually, everything runs together.

Why have the faculty sponsor name twice? Provide space for the name and the signature at the end to resolve this problem.

Limited space for signature. And if the signature is illegible, there is no corresponding printed name. Date indicator is repeated.

Digital Design University
Independent Study Course Proposal Form

Student Name _____ UID NO. _____

Mailing Address _____

_____

Email _____

Phone _____

College/School _____

Program _____

Academic Term (4 digit code) _____ Fall _____ Spring

Select One:
☐ Studio/Professional Elective
☐ Substitute for a required course/Course Name and Number

_____ # of credits

Faculty Sponsor's Name _____
Faculty: Please complete or insure the accuracy of the following items

Title and objectives of study or experience (include previous and related course study):

Procedures of study or nature of experience:

Nature of contact with faculty sponsor or supervisor:

Criteria for assessing student performance:

Student Signature _____ Date _____

Advisor Signature _____ Date _____

Faculty Sponsor Signature _____ Date _____

Dept. Chair Signature _____ Date _____

College/School Name _____ Date _____

Design principles applied to this example are:

- Alignment
- Hierarchy
- Repetition
- Grouping/Proximity
- Consistency
- White space

Brand identity addressed.
Clarity of title of form.

Hierarchy of content established with horizontal rules and headers. Provides visual impact and organization.

Numerical information clearly indicated with separated lines for writing each number. When making the fillable PDF form, you can use the comb setting for individual number blocks that will align with these dashed lines.

Name of faculty sponsor moved to approvals section.

Name and signature indicators with clarity of where to print and sign the approvals.

DDU Digital Design University
Independent Study Course Proposal Form

Student Information

Last Name

First Name

UID# __ __ __ __ __ – __ __ __ __

Academic Program Code __ __ __ __ __

Academic Term *(4 digit code)*   Fall __ __ __ __   Spring __ __ __ __

Email

Phone __ __ __ – __ __ __ – __ __ __ __

Current Mailing Address

Street   *City*   *State*   *Zip*

Course Information

# of Credits _____

Select One: ○ Studio/Professional Elective   ○ Substitute for a Required Course
○ Free Elective

Course Number __ __ __ __ __ __ __

Course Name

Faculty Sponsor
Faculty: Please complete or insure the accuracy of the following items.

Title and objectives of study or experience
(include previous and related course study):

Nature of contact with faculty sponsor or supervisor:

Procedures of study or nature of experience:

Criteria for assessing student performance:

Approvals
Name *(Please print clearly)*   Signature   Date

Student

Faculty Sponsor

Academic Advisor

Dept./Program Chair

Interactive PDF Form

The Portable Document Format (PDF) is the open file standard that allows for the exchange of electronic documents independent of any application software, hardware, or operating system. PDFs can contain multimedia elements such as links and buttons, form fields, audio, and video. Electronic signatures and various security settings are also an option.

PDF forms can be used for a variety of documents including:

- online publications
- presentations
- job applications
- tax forms
- conference registrations
- purchase orders

A PDF form makes it easier for the user to fill in the necessary information in the document without having to print it. It can then be submitted electronically by email or other file sharing methods. All forms should have an objective to achieve by gathering information through user input.

You can create a PDF in a variety of software, then add form fields and other interaction within Adobe Acrobat. Adobe InDesign also allows you to create and export an interactive PDF form. One limitation with using InDesign to create the interactive fields is that you cannot change the font for the text fields. But you can change fonts in Acrobat.

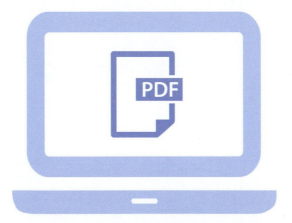

Interactivity within a PDF

PDF forms can integrate a variety of interactive elements:

- **Form fields**
  - ◊ Text field
  - ◊ Check box
  - ◊ Radio button
  - ◊ List box
  - ◊ Drop-down
  - ◊ Digital signature
  - ◊ Barcode
- **Interactivity**
  - ◊ Link
  - ◊ Button
  - ◊ Multimedia
    - Video
    - Sound
    - SWF
    - 3D
- **Cross references**
- **Actions**
  - ◊ Navigate
  - ◊ Submission of form
  - ◊ Print form

Radio buttons should be used when allowing only one option to select from a list of choices.

My favorite color is:

- ◎ Blue
- ◉ Red
- ◎ Purple
- ◎ Orange
- ◎ Green
- ◎ Yellow

Check boxes allow one or more options to be elected from a group.

What genre of magazines
do you like to read?

- ☐ Cooking
- ☐ Sports
- ☑ Fashion
- ☐ Crafts
- ☑ Travel
- ☐ News

A checklist for designing mobile input fields can be found at *www.nngroup.com/articles/mobile-input-checklist/.*

Web Forms

Web forms have various purposes such as

- surveys
- collection of data
- search mechanisms
- account creation
- login function
- e-commerce

The design needs to be simple, effective, and avoid other visual distractions. A user needs to have trust and confidence with the experience. Avoid the following:

- Asking for the same or similar information more than one time
- Asking for irrelevant information (not related to task at hand)
- Lengthy pop-up and drop-down menus
- Forcing users to fill out information unless absolutely necessary

Example of a basic web input form.

DDU

Create your account:

Name

Email

Confirm Email

Password

Must be at least six letters and one number.

Re-enter Password

SUBMIT

Form Elements

Standard graphical user interface elements should be used when designing forms.

- Text input fields
- Radio buttons
- Check boxes
- Text areas
- Submit buttons
- Drop-down selection menu
- Visual indicators for required information input versus optional information input
- Feedback (visual/verbal)

Error Indicators alert the user to problems with their form entries. Use visual and verbal feedback to notify the user of the problem. Avoid negativity by using positive wording for feedback and instructions.

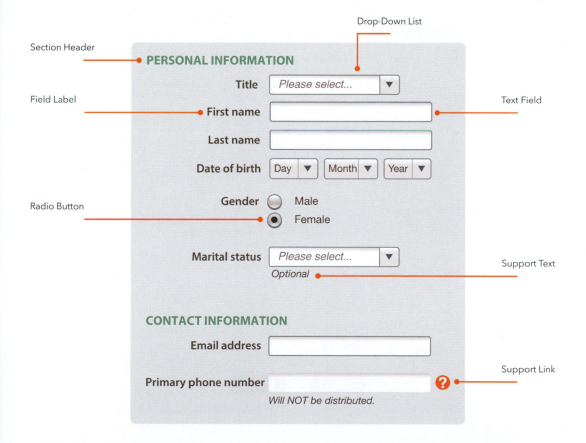

Chapter Exercise:
Creating an Interactive PDF Form

Let's go through the process of adding fields and buttons to a donation form. This exercise uses Adobe InDesign and Adobe Acrobat. InDesign allows you to create a variety of documents for use on screen and in print. You should already be familiar with InDesign to complete this exercise.

Part 1: Creating the PDF File

1. Download and decompress the **Chapter_07.zip** folder to your desktop. The folder contains the text and images needed to complete the exercise.

2. In the Chapter Folder open the file called **Donation_Form_Chptr07.indd**

3. The layout will appear as follows:

4. Go to the menu and choose **File > Export.**
   Save as: **Form_07_Int**
   Format: **Adobe PDF (Print)**

You do not need to use the Interactive PDF choice because you are adding the interaction in Acrobat.

Part 2: Inserting Text Fields

1. Open the new PDF file in **Adobe Acrobat**. In the right-hand column menu, select **Tools > Forms > Edit.**

2. When this message box appears, select **NO.** You will be creating your own text fields for this exercise.

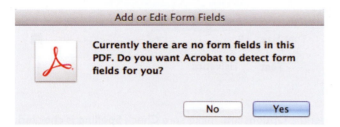

3. The menu header will say **Forms**, and the submenu is **Tasks.** Select **Add New Field** from the drop-down menu.

4. Create text fields on each of the white block areas – except for the **State** field. Be sure to change the **Field Name** to match the labels.

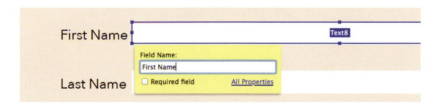

5. Select all the text fields (hold the Shift key and select the text fields) then right-click the mouse and select **Properties.**

Tip: You can right-click your mouse for a drop-down menu to select the field option.

6. Under the **Appearance** tab, change the **Font Size** to **9pt Helvetica.**

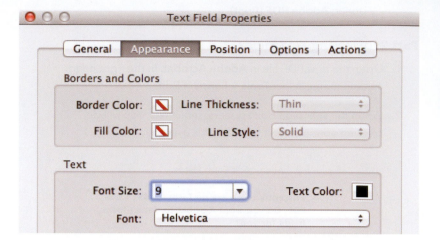

In the Properties box, under the Appearance tab, notice both the border color and fill color are set to none. This makes the fields transparent.

7. Under the **Options** tab, make sure **Check Spelling is checked** and deselect any other options. **Alignment** should be **Left.**

8. Now **Close** the Properties box.

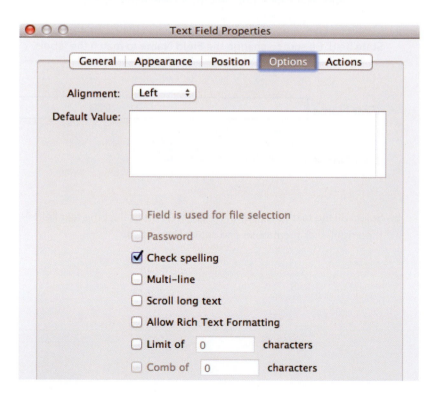

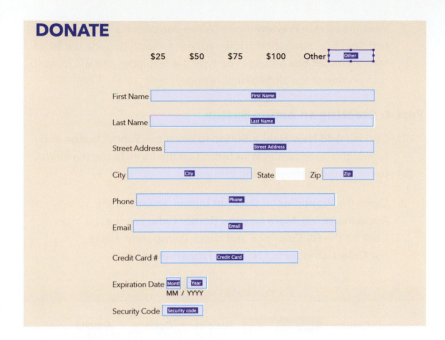

This is how your form will appear at this step in the exercise. All text fields have been set up, except the **State** field. You will be making a list box for this field.

Part 3: Creating a List Box

1. Click on **Add New Field > List Box** for the **State** text field. Name the field **State**. Then click on **All Properties.**

2. Under the **Appearance** tab, set the **Font** to **Helvetica, Size 9.**

3. Go to the **Options** tab. Here you will make a list of states using abbreviations. For the sake of time, just a few are needed to create the list example.

4. In the **Item** field: enter **AL** and then click **Add.** The AL will appear in the **Item List.** Continue to add a few more state abbreviations using the same process. Once you have 6 to 8 states in the list, you can **Close** the window.

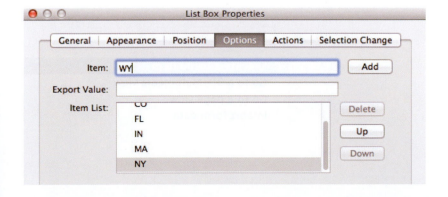

Once you have made the List Box, try your hand at a drop-down list as well. Then you can compare and see which you prefer for the form.

5. View the form in **Preview** mode. When you click inside the **State** text field box, navigation arrows appear to scroll through the list of states. This **list box** also lets you type the first letter and will jump to that portion of the alphabetical listing.

Part 4: Creating an Action Button

1. Choose **Add New Field > Button** to cover the **Submit button** and repeat the same for the **Print button** on the form. Name the fields to match the corresponding buttons.

2. Open the **Properties** for the **Print button** and select the **Appearance** tab. Make sure the **Border Color** is none. Click on the **Fill Color** box and check **Transparent.** Close the **Colors** window, but **NOT** the **Properties** window.

3. Open the **Actions** tab. **Select Trigger** should read **Mouse Up.** Under the **Select Action** drop-down menu, choose **Execute a menu item.**

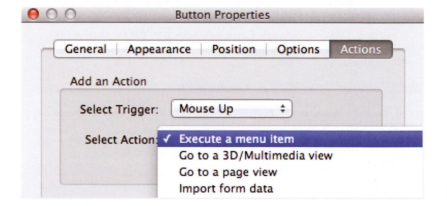

4. Click on the **Add button** and select **File > Print** and click **OK.**

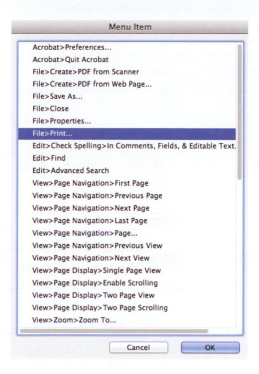

The Submit button does not have an actual link for this exercise. But if you want to try the steps to create a link, follow the same steps as the Print button, but under the **Actions** tab choose **Button Properties > Action > Submit a Form**. Click the **Add** button and another window will appear and ask you to **Enter a URL** for this link, **Export Format**, and **Field Selection**.

Part 5: Creating Radio Buttons

Next, you will create **Radio** buttons for the contribution dollar amounts.

1. Turn on **Rulers** in Acrobat by going to the menu **View > Show/Hide > Rulers & Grids > Rulers.** Drag grid/guide lines from the rulers onto the layout. Mark the row where the radio buttons will need to be placed.

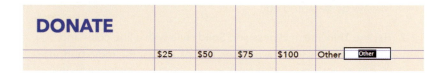

2. Once again, use the **Add Text Field** (or right-click your mouse for a drop-down menu to appear) and choose **Radio Button.**

3. You will be doing a group of radio buttons for the contribution amount selections. When the user selects a radio button, only one can be active at a time, thus limiting it to one final choice. Draw the button in front of $25. A yellow window will open as shown below:

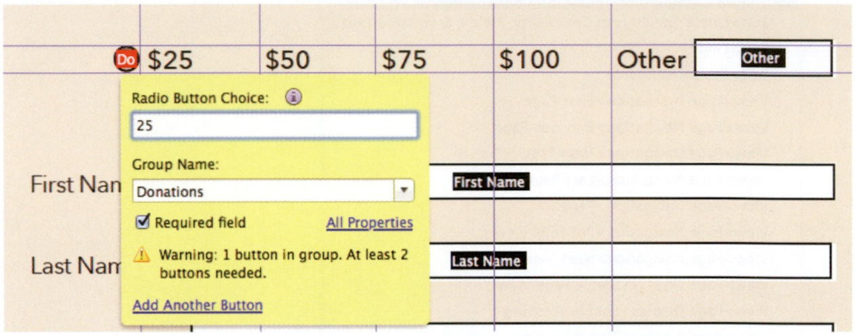

It is important when making a group of radio buttons that you use the **Add Another Button** in the yellow information window.

4. Name the **Button Choice** "**25**" (the dollar amount listed). The **Group Name** should be "**Donations.**" Check the **Required field** option so the check mark is turned on. Now click on **Add Another Button.**

5. Go through the same steps to make each additional radio button for each dollar amount. When the yellow information window opens, name the button with the corresponding dollar amount (50, 75, etc.) The **Group Name** must stay the same to work properly.

6. Select the **Radio buttons** and open **Properties**. Under the **Appearance** menu you can adjust the **Border a**nd **Fill** colors. You can also experiment with **Line Thickness** and **Line Style**. Close when done and use the **Preview** mode to view your changes. You can always go back and edit.

7. Try the **Thin** line thickness and **Solid** style with a line color and transparent fill. Preview and see the result. Test the radio buttons by clicking on them. Only one at a time will be marked with the center circle to indicate your selection.

8. Test your form in the **Preview** mode and try typing in the text fields to see if you like the font size. Again, you can go back to the **Edit** mode and make changes to your liking.

9. Remember to **Save** your file.

Summary

Form design has a variety of uses and must be adapted to both print and digital access and delivery. Visual design principles and organization of information should be integrated into all form design.

Key principles that the designer should follow are:

- Apply design principles of layout.
- Don't overload the form with unnecessary content.
- Limit the number of typefaces.
- Use PDF forms to allow for electronic delivery.

This completes the chapter. You should now be able to:

- Apply information design principles to form layout.
- Organize form content for effective communication.
- Design an interactive PDF form.

The next chapter focuses on publishing to mobile devices.

What is Digital Publishing?

8

Publishing to Mobile Devices

Digital Publishing is not a new concept. However, there has been a radical shift in the publishing industry to take advantage of the digital capabilities available to consumers. EPUB, or electronic publication, has been widely adopted by mobile readers using Kindles, Nooks, and iPads. Adobe InDesign allows you to design, produce, and package an unlimited number of eBooks for multiple devices.

This chapter explores how to publish content to digital devices, specifically the iPad. At the completion of this chapter, you will be able to:

- Describe digital publishing.

- Describe the difference between an eBook and an EPUB.

- Describe the difference between a fluid and a fixed layout.

- Discuss how to design for touch devices.

- List the types of gesture interactions for touch devices.

- Describe the InDesign EPUB workflow.

- Export a fixed EPUB layout for an EPUB reader.

What Is Digital Publishing?

Digital publishing, also known as electronic publishing, uses computer technology to produce and distribute content to users. As smartphone and tablet device sales continue to grow exponentially, people are reading, listening to music, watching videos, and playing games all on one device. Market research indicates that half of all major magazines and newspapers are delivering content digitally.

For more information on digital reading, check out Craig Mod's article, *Post Artifact Books and Publishing* at **craigmod.com/journal/post_artifact/**.

Examples of Digital Publishing

Digital publishing takes content in print, sound, and/or video and saves it into a format that can be accessed by computer technology. This encompasses a wide range of content in the form of:

- Books
- Magazines
- Newspapers
- Newsletters
- Journals
- Catalogs
- Databases

The content is published through digital media and can appear in a variety of formats. An EPUB can be published for the Amazon Kindle device and as an iBook for Apple devices. Mobile apps are designed for different operating systems, including Android and iOS. Content can be published and disseminated digitally through the use of:

- PDF
- EPUB
- Mobile Apps
- Web
- DVD
- CD-ROM

With an EPUB, you can design a fixed or reflowable electronic publication, allowing it to be viewed on various digital devices. Before you do this, it is important to understand what an EPUB is. Isn't it the same as an eBook? The answer is no. They are different.

The Difference between an eBook and an EPUB

At the end of this chapter, you will use Adobe InDesign to export an eBook as an EPUB file. What is the difference between an eBook and an EPUB? An **eBook** is simply any electronic book that can be read on digital devices such as a desktop or laptop computer. This can be exported in a variety of formats including PDF and HTML.

For more information about the International Digital Publishing Forum (IDPF) and the development and promotion of electronic publishing, visit *http://idpf.org*.

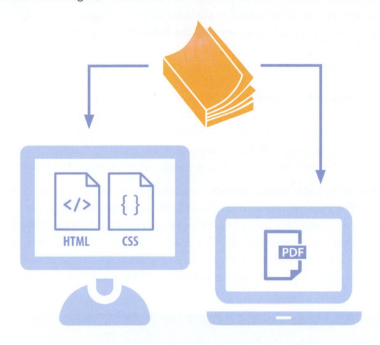

An **EPUB** is specific type of eBook. It is an actual open formatting standard developed by the International Digital Publishing Forum (IDPF). It requires an EPUB reader to view, such as iBooks for Apple devices. An EPUB is actually a zipped file with an .epub extension. The compressed package contains HTML or XHTML, CSS files, linked images and fonts, folders, and some XML files. An EPUB is essentially a website.

An EPUB is a group of files that are bundled together and uses the .epub file extension.

Choosing an EPUB Layout

Let's review. The EPUB content is packaged into a single file so that it can be distributed and sold electronically. EPUB files can be viewed using an EPUB reader on the Kindle, Nook, and Apple and Android devices. In addition, the exported publications can be separated into two categories, reflowable formats and fixed layout formats. With the ever-evolving digital industry, you should take time to consider which publication would benefit from either the fixed layout format or the reflowable format.

First, let's define each format.

- **Fixed layout formats** are displayed in the same way the layout would appear if printed. All of the content – images, words, paragraphs, and columns – remain in a fixed position within a specific page size. An extra bonus is the ability to incorporate video, audio, and interactivity. This is similar to an interactive PDF file.

- **Reflowable layout formats** are adaptable on various screen sizes. The content adjusts and reflows to fit the screen size. The user can control the look of the content by choosing the font family, font size, margin size, and line spacing to make the reading more comfortable. Think of this layout as one long linear flow of text with anchored graphics, similar to HTML or a Microsoft Word document.

A reflowable EPUB allows readers to change the font family and size of the text. A fixed EPUB maintains the design integrity of the publication.

Fixed layouts work best for designers. The format preserves your original design on each page. If your publication includes a large number of graphics, audio, and video content, use a fixed layout. Examples of fixed EPUB layouts include children's book, cookbooks, and graphic novels. A downside to using a fixed layout is distribution. Kindle devices do not support this format and you are pretty much limited to tablet devices. You, as the designer, are in complete control of the user experience.

Reflowable EPUBs put the user in control of the content to provide them with an optimal reading experience for text-based documents. If your publication is text-heavy with few graphics, use a reflowable layout. Examples of reflowable EPUBs include trade books (fiction and non-fiction books) and journals. The reflowable format is the most common and widely distributed layout for eBooks. The downside is that this format does not preserve the integrity of the layout and design.

Empathize with Your EPUB Readers

Creating an EPUB is more than just taking a print layout and exporting it into a digital format. You still need to use your design components: grids, visual organization and hierarchy, typography, imagery, and color. As mentioned in previous chapters, you should always start your digital design by thinking about your intended audience and the final delivery.

For more info on which reading devices work with the various file formats and advice about designing digital books:

www.e-ink-info.com/devices
www.thebookdesigner.com

The most popular platforms for EPUBs include the Amazon Kindle, the Apple iBooks App, the Barnes & Noble Nook, and the Kobo eReader.

User Options for EPUB Layouts	FIXED	REFLOWABLE
Adapts to screen size change.		X
Alter orientation – portrait vs. landscape	X	
Imagery stays at a fixed size	X	
User can change type size, font, line spacing		X
Users can interact, watch video, sync audio	X	
Kindle supported		X

Designing for Touch

Let's take a quick detour to understand the respective limitations and capabilities of both the target user and the digital device you are designing for. Where do we begin? Since the published content will be displayed on a touch device, let's start designing for fingers and, especially, thumbs.

A user physically interacts with a smartphone or tablet device by tapping on it. This is a form of direct manipulation. A key factor to remember is that a touch gesture does not have the same accuracy as a mouse click. You must increase the touch target sizes and spaces for images, links, and buttons to reduce user errors. So, how big should you create your buttons and links?

- Apple recommends a touch target size of at least 44 x 44 pixels.
- Google recommends a touch target size of 48 pixels.
- Microsoft suggests 34 pixels with a minimum touch target size of 26 pixels for the UI controls.

A mouse cursor can easily point and click on smaller buttons and links. Fingers are not as accurate. Target sizes must be big enough to record the touch action.

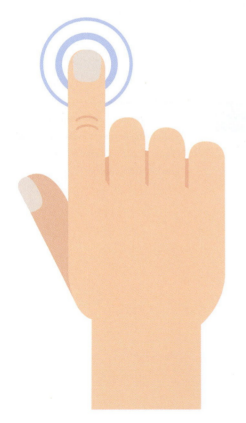

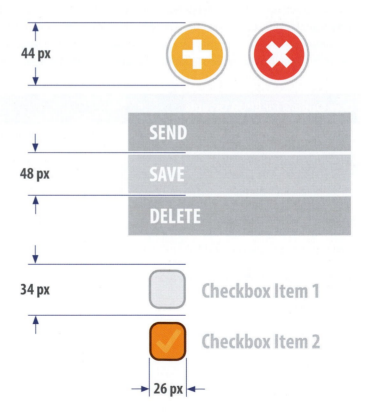

Understanding Mobile Ergonomics

Ergonomics focuses on designing for people and optimizing how they interact with products. This plays a crucial role in creating an efficient layout for your digital publication. Think about the ways you hold and interact with a mobile device. The most common ways include:

- One handed using a thumb to tap
- Both hands and both thumbs to tap
- One hand to hold the device and the other hand's index finger to tap

Don't stop with the user's hands; think about their overall posture. A user can be sitting up at a table or on a bus. Users can be reclining on a sofa or bed with the device resting on their chest or held overhead. No matter what position, place your interactive controls where they can provide the most effective functionality and ease of use.

For more information on mobile device ergonomics, read Steven Hoober study from 2013, *How Do Users Really Hold Mobile Devices*, at ***www.uxmatters.com/mt/archives/2013/02/how-do-users-really-hold-mobile-devices.php.***

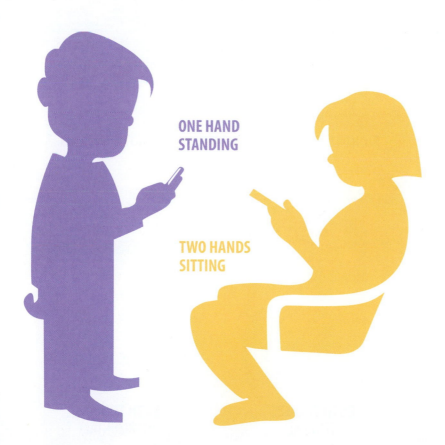

Designing for Thumbs and the Obtrusive Hand

When planning your digital publication's user interface, place your UI buttons based on where the user's fingers can easily access the screen. For thumbs, position navigational buttons near the bottom or down the sides of the user interface; it makes them easier to reach. Don't forget to design for two device orientations: vertical and horizontal.

Obviously the hand is a much larger direct manipulator than a mouse cursor. As a result, part of the screen is hidden underneath the hand while the user is tapping or gesturing. Be mindful of this as you design your content and feedback for the user. Avoid displaying visual feedback below the controls.

Position your buttons in the easiest-to-reach areas on the device. The bottom and sides are the easiest to tap with a thumb. Anything placed in the middle or the top of the screen requires more effort to reach it.

PHONE

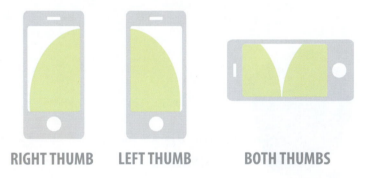

RIGHT THUMB **LEFT THUMB** **BOTH THUMBS**

TABLET

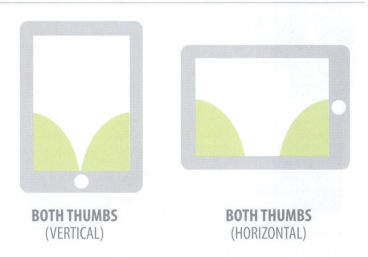

BOTH THUMBS
(VERTICAL)

BOTH THUMBS
(HORIZONTAL)

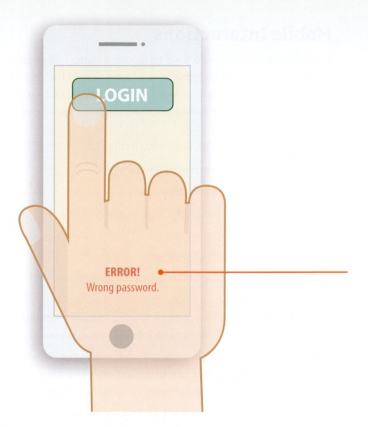

Be mindful of the obstructing hand. Avoid placing visual feedback below any UI controls.

The user may not see or may miss this feedback because the hand is blocking it.

Place your UI buttons based on where the fingers can easily reach the screen on the device.

Mobile Interactions

How many times have you tried to tap on a button on your smartphone only to activate the button that was placed next to the one you wanted? Developing interactivity that is controlled through human gestures is becoming part of the basic toolsets a designer must know and design for.

Mobile users interact with the content through:

- Touching the screen with their finger
- Tapping the screen with a stylus
- Entering information through buttons or keypads

Some common gestures include:

- **Tap:** The pressure of the user's finger activates an interface button or link.
- **Tap and Drag:** This gesture is used to push elements around on the screen. An example is to drag and move an app icon.
- **Swipe:** This gesture adds a directional movement to the tap. A swipe is typically used to access on-screen menus or move through content presented in a slideshow format.
- **Pinch:** This gesture uses two fingers to control zooming in and out of a screen.

Multitouch gestures let you use several fingers to interact with touch pads or devices. Some common gestures include tap, swipe, pinch, and flick.

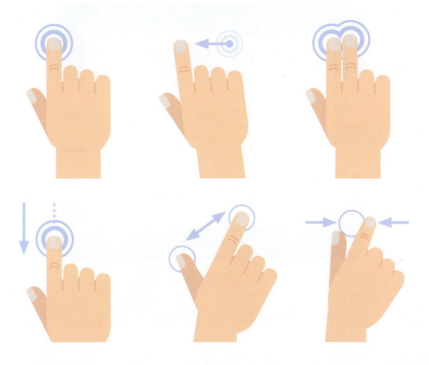

Moving through the Content

So how does tapping or swiping affect the flow of content? Equally important to mobile interactivity is understanding how your reader can actually choose to read the content on a device. There are various models for delivering and navigating through digital content. These navigation models include:

- **Slideshow:** This linear model is similar to pages in a printed book. A PDF document or a fixed layout EPUB is a good example.

- **Scroll:** This model delivers the content vertically or horizontally in one continuous linear structure. Think of an HTML web page.

- **Clothesline:** This model is used by the Adobe Digital Publishing Solution (DPS) to build mobile apps by stringing different InDesign documents together. The reader can swipe up and down to read one document or side to side to read the other documents.

More information about Adobe's Digital Publishing Solution can be found at **www.adobe.com/products/ digital-publishing-solution.html.**

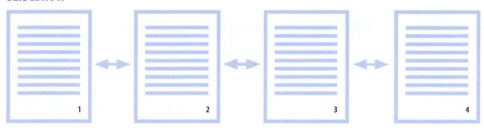

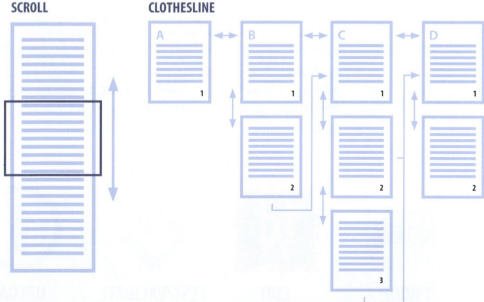

Using Adobe InDesign to Create an EPUB

Adobe put digital publishing on the map by making content accessible via technology. Starting in the early 1990s with the Portable Document Format (PDF), Adobe has grown and now offers many new ways to publish content digitally. Starting with Adobe InDesign CC 2014, you can now easily export an EPUB 3 publication in both a fixed or reflowable format. Wait. *What is EPUB 3?*

EPUB 3 Specification

An EPUB is the XML format for digital books and electronic publications. The International Digital Publishing Forum (IDPF) is the standards-making body for EPUBs, similar to the World Wide Web Consortium (W3C) for the Web. The format follows certain specifications and standards. At the time of this writing, **EPUB 3** is the latest version of these standards and embraces HTML5 and CSS3. This means that EPUBs can now contain audio, video, and interactivity just like modern websites.

EPUB Workflow Using Adobe InDesign

It is important to understand InDesign's EPUB workflow in order to produce and distribute digital content. Here is the general idea:

- **Adobe InDesign:** Design the layout and format the content for the EPUB export. InDesign lets you export both fixed or reflowable EPUB formats.

- **Adobe Digital Editions:** This free eReader allows you to proof your EPUB on your desktop or laptop during the development stage. If revisions are needed, simply go back to InDesign, make the changes, then export to EPUB again and preview it again.

- **EpubCheck:** This is an open source tool on the GitHub website that helps validate your publication to ensure it meets the requirements of the EPUB 3 standards.

- **Upload:** Distribute your eBook to online stores for purchase.

More information about EPUB 3 can be found at *epubzone.org/epub-3-overview/understanding-epub-3.*

The EPUB workflow is an iterative process. You must confirm that your EPUB passes a validation check. When your EPUB validates, you can begin the publishing process to get it into the iBooks store, Barnes & Noble, or convert it to Kindle eBook format so it can be sold at Amazon.

DESIGN → **PROOF** → **EDIT** → **TEST/VALIDATE** → **UPLOAD**

Chapter Exercise:
Creating a Fixed Layout EPUB

Let's take a look at digital publishing in action. This exercise uses Adobe InDesign to build a simple fixed layout EPUB for an iPad. To complete this exercise you need Adobe InDesign CC 2014 or later. The content for the EPUB is a children's picture book about dinosaurs. This publication includes a large number of graphics and an audio file.

Download and uncompress the **Chapter_08.zip** folder to your desktop. The folder contains all the files needed to complete this exercise. Feel free to substitute your own images and text.

PART 1: Creating a Digital Publishing Document

Adobe InDesign allows you to create and export a document to EPUB to allow your users to view the content in an EPUB reader. The setup is simple to do. Make sure you have version CC 2014 or later.

1. In Adobe InDesign, choose **File > New > Document**.

2. The New Document dialog box appears. Change the **Intent** to **Digital Publishing**. The default page size is automatically set to an iPad with a horizontal orientation.

3. Change the **Number of Pages** from **1** to **8** for the new document.

4. Uncheck the check box for **Primary Text Frame**. This option adds a text frame on the master page. You do not need this for the EPUB you are designing.

Download the exercise file to your hard drive:

www.routledge.com/cw/Jackson

Chapter_08.zip

More information about Adobe InDesign can be found at *helpx.adobe.com/indesign/how-to/indesign-prepare-document-for-epub.html*.

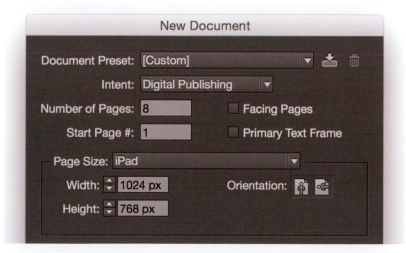

5. Change the number of columns to **6** and set the gutter to **20 pixels**.

6. Click **OK** to create the EPUB document.

7. Make sure the first page is active. Select **File > Place**. In the Place dialog box, browse to select the file in the **images** folder named **FrontCover.jpg** and then click **Open**. Center the image on the page.

For EPUB design, images should be saved in JPEG or PNG format, preferably in JPEG format. If you need transparency in the image, save it as a PNG. The downside to this format is that it takes longer to process and may impact the user experience, depending on how much RAM your readers have in their iPads.

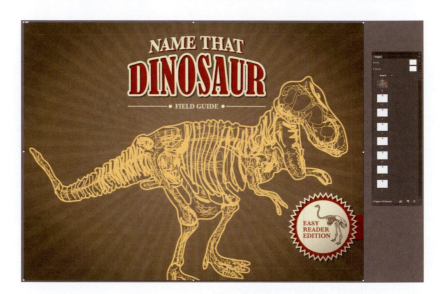

When exporting the EPUB, the text is not rasterized. The live text is searchable and selectable. Hyperlinks on text are supported to URLs, text anchors, and pages. Kerning is not supported. OpenType features, including small caps, all caps, and fractions are not supported due to limited device support.

8. Design the remaining pages in the EPUB. Use the provided images and text. You can also open the completed **DinoPUB.indd** file located in the **Completed** folder in the downloaded **Chapter_08** folder to follow along or modify.

Apatosaurus.png

AudioButton.eps

BackCover.jpg

DinoPageGraphic.eps

Here are the designed pages from the completed **DinoPUB.indd** file that you can use for reference. Feel free to substitute you own images and text.

Stegosaurus

The Stegosaurus lived 150 million years ago. It was a plant eater and featured rows of hard plates along its back and tail.

An adult Stegosaurus was around 30 feet in length, 14 feet in height and weighed nearly 5 metric tons.

Tyrannosaurus Rex

The Tyrannosaurus was one of the largest meat eating dinosaurs. It lived in an area of the world that is now North America.

The Tyrannosaurus measured up 42 feet in length, and could weigh up to 7 tons. Many scientists believe it could run at a speed of around 25 miles per hour.

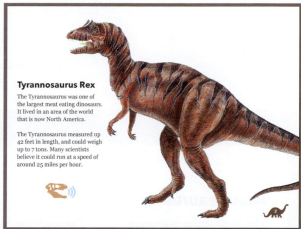

Triceratops

The Triceratops was a plant eating dinosaur. It horns were used to protect itself from the meat eating Tyrannosaurus Rex.

An adult Triceratops was about 26 feet in length, 10 feet in height, and weighed anywhere between 6 to 12 tons.

Corythosaurus

The Corythosaurus lived about 76-65 million years ago. It had a hollow, bony crest on top of its head. The Corythosaurus was a plant eater, eating pine needles, leaves, and twigs.

An adult Corythosaurus grew to be about 33 feet long. It weighed about 5 tons and walked and ran on two legs.

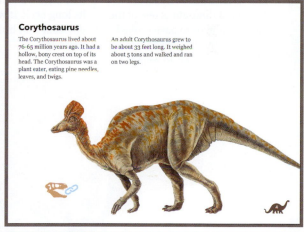

Apatosaurus

The Apatosaurus is also well known as the Brontosaurus. This giant dinosaur is one of the largest animals to have walked on Earth, reaching an 75 feet in length and 23 tons in weight.

The Apatosaurus had a long tail that helped balanced its body with its long neck. It was a plant eating dinosaur that lived 150 million years ago.

Velociraptor

The Velociraptor lived about 73 million years ago. It was a meat eater and thought to have killed its prey with sharp claws on its rear feet.

An adult Velociraptor could grow up to 6 feet in length and weigh up to 33 pounds.

PART 2: Previewing the EPUB

You can preview your InDesign document using the **EPUB Interactivity Preview** panel. This panels gives you a rough idea of how the EPUB will look and function on the iPad.

1. To preview the EPUB document, select **Window > Interactive > EPUB Interactivity Preview**. Scale the panel up to see the preview controls better in the window.

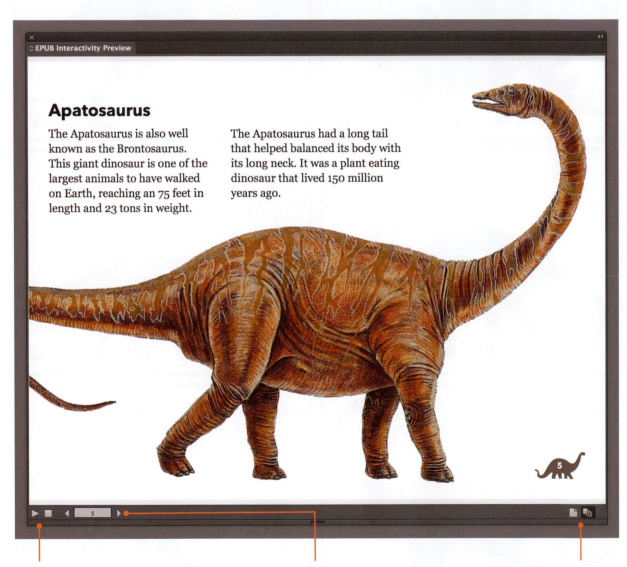

Click the arrow to play the preview of the document. Click the square to clear the preview.

Click the left and right arrows to navigate between previous and next pages.

Click to set the mode to preview spread mode or to preview the entire document mode.

PART 3: Adding Interactivity to the EPUB

As you learned in Chapter 7, InDesign allows you to add buttons, multi-state objects, and form fields to create interactive PDF files. Starting with Adobe InDesign CC 2014, you also have the ability to add interactivity to your fixed-layout EPUB exports. Let's see how it works.

1. To access the interactive features you can add to your document, change the **Workspace** to **Digital Publishing**. This displays the interactive and animation panels that you will need to complete this part of the exercise.

2. Go to the **Corythosaurus** page in your document. If you have not imported the **LinkButton.eps** graphic, do so.

3. While the graphic is still selected, click on the **Buttons and Forms** tab to open it.

4. Click the **Convert Object To A Button** icon in the Buttons panel. You can also choose **Object > Interactive > Convert to Button**.

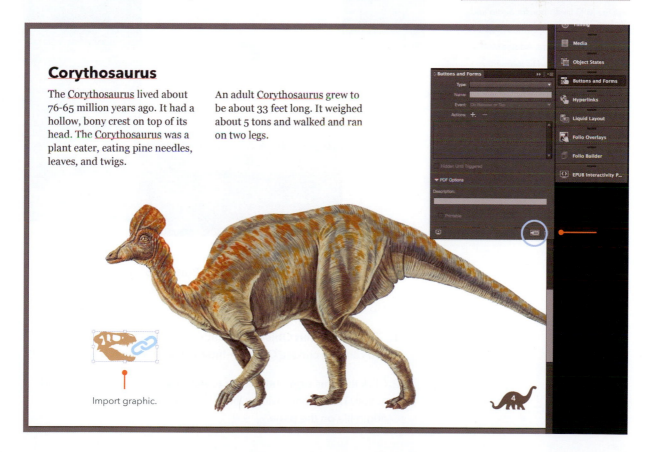

Import graphic.

5. You can assign actions to the button for different events. For example, you can create an action that opens a URL when clicked or tapped. Click the **plus sign** button next to **Actions**, and choose the **Go To URL** action.

6. Specify the following web page address: *http://www. amnh.org/exhibitions/permanent-exhibitions/fossil-halls/ hall-of-ornithischian-dinosaurs/corythosaurus*.

7. Go to the **Tyrannosaurus Rex** page in your document.

8. Choose **File > Place** and locate the MP3 file in the **audio** folder. You will see an empty box appear. What is this? It is a placeholder for your audio file.

9. While the object is still selected, open the **Media** panel. Check the check box for **Stop on Page Turn**.

When working with digital media files, use the MP3 file format for audio and the MP4 file format for video. It needs to be H.264 encoded. Adobe Media Encoder can be used to format the media files

10. If you have not imported the **AudioButton.eps** graphic, do so. While the graphic is still selected, click on the **Buttons and Forms** tab to open it.

11. Click the **Convert Object To A Button** icon in the Buttons panel. You can also choose **Object > Interactive > Convert to Button**.

12. Click the **plus sign** button next to **Actions**, and choose the **Sound** action. The MP3 file will be linked automatically since it is the only audio file on the page.

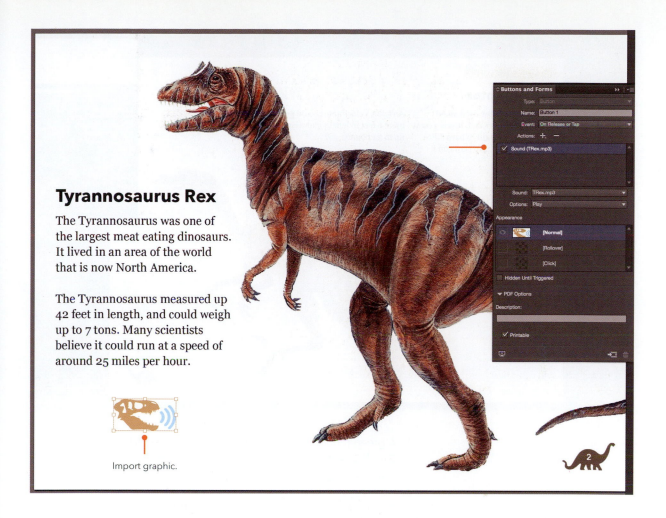

Tyrannosaurus Rex

The Tyrannosaurus was one of the largest meat eating dinosaurs. It lived in an area of the world that is now North America.

The Tyrannosaurus measured up 42 feet in length, and could weigh up to 7 tons. Many scientists believe it could run at a speed of around 25 miles per hour.

Import graphic.

PART 4: Adding Animation to the EPUB

Adobe InDesign also allows you to add animation effects that move objects in your exported EPUB files. For example, you can apply a motion preset to an image that makes it appear to fly in from the left side of the screen. Let's animate the Velociraptor. It is very easy to do.

1. Go to the **Velociraptor** page in your document.

2. Select the dinosaur illustration that will animate on the page.

3. Click on the **Animation** tab (**Window > Interactive > Animation**), and choose the **Fly In From Left** motion preset from the Preset menu. Motion presets are pre-made animations that you can apply to objects quickly.

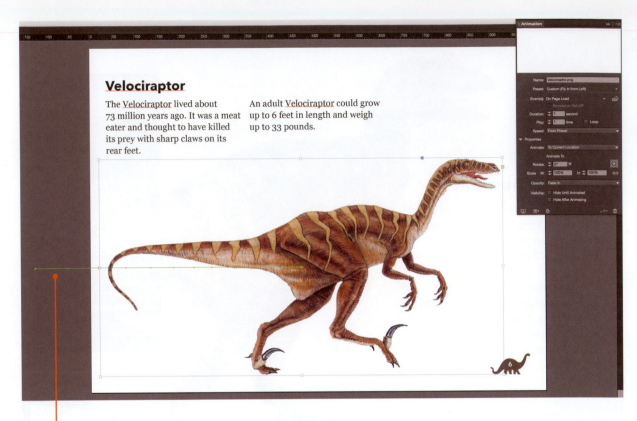

Velociraptor

The Velociraptor lived about 73 million years ago. It was a meat eater and thought to have killed its prey with sharp claws on its rear feet.

An adult Velociraptor could grow up to 6 feet in length and weigh up to 33 pounds.

Motion path

More information about downloading Adobe Digital Editions can be found at *www.adobe.com/solutions/ebook/ digital-editions.html*.

4. A green motion path appears next to the selected object. Use the Direct Selection tool and the Pen tool to edit a motion path using the same method you use to edit a path.

5. Preview the added interactions and animation in the **EPUB Interactivity Preview** panel.

PART 5: Exporting the Fixed Layout EPUB

Now that you have added the interactions and animations, it is time to export the EPUB. You can export the document or book as a reflowable or fixed layout EPUB that is compatible with the eBook reader software.

1. Save your current Adobe InDesign file. Choose **File > Save**.

2. Choose **File > Export**.

3. Specify a filename as **DinoEPUB** and set a location.

4. From the **Save as Type** list, choose **EPUB (Fixed Layout)**, and then click **Save**.

5. In the EPUB Export Options dialog box, specify the exported file to include a cover image. Use the first page to create the cover image. The thumbnail is used to depict the book in the EPUB readers or the Adobe Digital Editions Reader library view.

6. Add the appropriate metadata such as the title for the EPUB.

7. To view the file, you need an EPUB reader. You can use the Adobe Digital Editions software, which you can download free from the Adobe website. On a Mac, you can also use the iBooks app.

8. Click **OK** to create the EPUB file.

Adobe InDesign creates a single .epub file containing the XHTML-based content. Once you have tested the EPUB file, the next step is to make sure that the EPUB is valid. What does that mean? Basically it means that your EPUB adheres to all of the standards provided by the International Digital Publishing Forum (IDPF) for EPUB 3. Use **EpubCheck** on the GitHub website to validate your publication to ensure it meets all requirements.

More information about downloading EpubCheck can be found at *https://github.com/IDPF/epubcheck.*

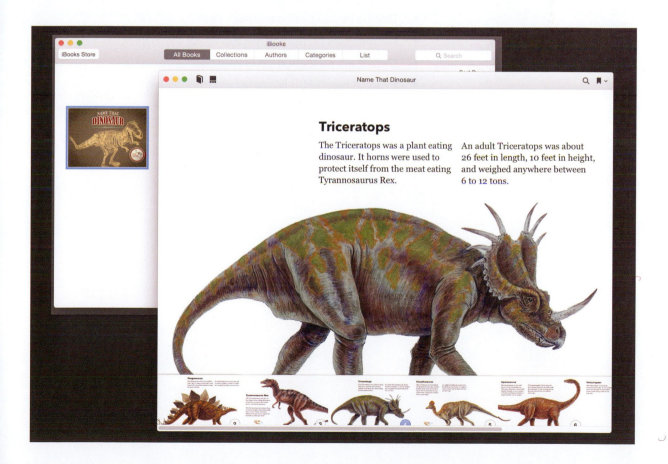

Summary

This chapter explored how to design EPUB documents for mobile devices. Adobe InDesign allows you to create and export a document to either a fixed or reflowable EPUB format. The reflowable format is better suited for text-driven documents such as trade books. Also, the reflowable format allows the reader to change the font and size of the text in the reader.

The fixed layout format allows you to include audio, video, and Edge Animate content in your EPUB documents. You can also export interactivity that includes controls such as buttons, animations, and hyperlinks to the fixed layout format. It is better suited for children's books, cookbooks, and graphic novels.

This completes this chapter. You should now be able to:

- Describe digital publishing.
- Describe the difference between an eBook and an EPUB.
- Describe the difference between a fluid and a fixed layout.
- Discuss how to design for touch devices.
- List the types of gesture interactions for touch devices.
- Describe the InDesign EPUB workflow.
- Export a fixed EPUB layout for an EPUB reader.

The next chapter focuses on visual storytelling techniques.

9

Understanding Visual Storytelling

What makes a good story? A good story needs a compelling plot that involves appealing characters living in a believable world. Understanding story and its structure is important, but you are working in a visual medium. As a visual storyteller, you can enhance a story's emotional experience by showing how a story unfolds through a sequence of images.

Understanding the story structure and how to visualize it is the topic of this chapter. At the completion of this chapter, you will be able to:

- Describe the components that make up a good story.
- Build a composition that keeps the audience visually interested in a story.
- Discuss how lines, shapes, colors, and values are used together to form a composition.
- Create unique and compelling characters for animation.
- Use different camera shots to "show" the story.
- Apply visual storytelling techniques to create a storyboard for a short animation.

Anatomy of a Story

Stories always start with an idea. Ideas can come from all around you from your imagination, personal observations, life experiences, to your dreams and nightmares. These random thoughts or observations are recorded as events. Events are then woven together to formulate the story's plot.

The **plot** is not the story itself; it is all of the action that takes place during the story. How the action affects the characters physically and emotionally builds a good story. The fundamental components of any story involve a character or characters in a setting, a conflict that causes change, and a resolution that depicts the consequences of the character's actions.

A good story is judged by the emotional impact it has on its audience. Adding interest to your story triggers this emotional response. Audiences want to be able to relate to the characters. Once bonded, audience members experience the turmoil the characters go through by projecting themselves into the story. Audiences also anticipate the dramatic tension created by the conflict and want to know what is going to happen next.

ACT 1: BEGINNING	ACT 2: MIDDLE	ACT 3: END

Exposition → Conflict → Rising Tension → Climax → Resolution

The dramatic story structure determines when events will happen in a story.

Without any emotional involvement, a story is reduced to a series of events. The dramatic structure consists of a beginning, middle, and an end. Each act applies just the right amount of dramatic tension at the right time and in the right place.

Chapter 9 | Understanding Visual Storytelling

- **Act One** is called exposition and it gives the audience information in order to understand a story. It introduces the setting, the characters, their goals, and the conflicting situation that the story is about.

- **Act Two** focuses on the conflict. It drives the story forward raising the tension. The tension reaches a high point at the end of Act Two. This is also referred to as the climax or turning point, when the plot changes for better or for worse for the hero. During this moment, the hero takes action and brings the story to a conclusion.

- **Act Three** is the resolution and end of the story. It resolves the conflicts that have arisen. Act Three ties together the loose ends of the story and allows the audience to learn what happened to the characters after the conflict is resolved. This is often referred to as closure.

For more information on visual storytelling, read *The Visual Story: Creating the Visual Structure of Film, TV and Digital Media* by Bruce Block.

Make Every Scene Count

Creating beautiful imagery is not enough if the visuals do not reinforce the story's narrative or meet the audience's expectations. For each scene in your story, you need to visually answer the following three questions that audience members ask:

- **What is going on?**

- **Who is involved?**

- **How should I feel?**

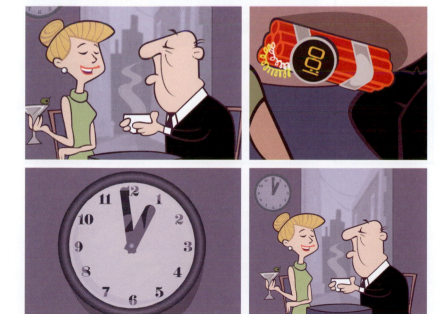

Alfred Hitchcock strongly believed in giving his audience just the right amount of visual information to get them involved with the story. His "bomb theory" is widely referenced as a good visual storytelling technique in building suspense.

Composing the Space

Every shot in a film is about something, from two characters talking to revealing an object of significant importance. A cinematographer chooses how to frame a shot using the camera's relative distance from the subject, its angle, and movement. When framing a shot, cinematographers position the actors, props, and lights in a way that is aesthetically pleasing to them and hopefully to the audience.

The Rule of Thirds

As a visual storyteller, you must keep the audience visually interested in the scene. How you compose the scene is completely up to you. Some compositions are more effective than others. Building a good composition is not an exact science. Do some research.

When you watch a film or animation, ask yourself the following questions:

- What grabs your attention first in a scene?
- What do you notice after that?
- What guides your eye around to the most interesting part?

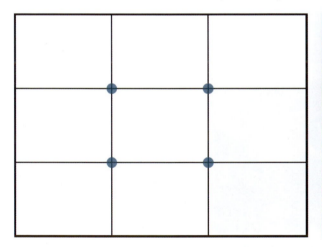

The Rule of Thirds can help you create engaging, dynamic scenes.

Your imagery should encourage your audience to scan the frame, seeking out what is most important. **The Rule of Thirds** is a compositional guideline that can help. The concept behind this is to divide the frame horizontally and vertically into thirds. The image is divided into nine equal parts by four straight lines, two equally spaced horizontal lines and two equally spaced vertical lines.

The important compositional element is positioned at the intersection of two lines. Actually any one of the four points of intersection highlighted is a strong place for a point of interest. What about the center? It is compositionally acceptable to center characters when they directly face the audience. If a character is facing in profile, it should be positioned about a third of the way across the shot. The character should look into a space wider than the space behind it. This is referred to as **lead room**.

Take a look at the image below. The left image shows a lack of headroom resulting in an unconformable composition. We feel like the man is going to hit his head on the top of the frame. The middle image provides too much headroom and the character appears to fall out of the frame. The right image illustrates proper headroom by providing just enough open space above the man's head.

Without proper lead room, the audience perceives the character as boxed in, with no place to go.

Make sure you provide enough headroom for your character.

Positioning the Horizon Line

The horizon line should never be in the center of the composition where it divides the composition in half. If the frame is split into two equal halves, there is no tension generated. The composition appears weak and uninteresting to the audience. Each half of the frame visually communicates different emotional connotations.

Each half of the frame communicates different emotional connotations.

The top half of a composition implies a feeling of freedom, aspiration or accomplishment. Characters placed in the top half of a composition dominate the shot. The bottom half suggests a "heavier," oppressed feeling. Characters placed in the lower half of a composition look and feel dominated or constrained.

Try to balance the elements of the composition. Make sure the top or sides of the shot do not appear visually "heavier" than the bottom or the opposite side. If you are going to follow any rule regarding composition, the best one to follow is to keep it simple.

For more information on visual storytelling, read *Graphic Storytelling and Visual Narrative* by Will Eisner.

Chapter 9 | Understanding Visual Storytelling

Using Lines and Shapes

Design elements such as line, shape, color, and value are used together to form a composition. Each element conveys a certain message. When combined together, they evoke an emotional response from the audience. Let's look at these elements of visual design in more detail.

Lines

Lines are a good place to start because they are the most basic element of design. They imply movement and direct the viewer's eye within a frame. Lines can be horizontal, vertical, or diagonal.

Each line orientation generates a different psychological and emotional reaction from the audience:

- **Horizontal lines** convey a sense of stability, restfulness, or calm. Most of us associate horizontal lines with the horizon or a floor, something stable that we can walk on without the risk of falling down. When we go to sleep at night, we lie down in a horizontal position.

- **Vertical lines** convey strength and power. Compared to horizontal lines, vertical lines are more dynamic, active, and tend to dominate the scene.

- **Diagonal lines** imply motion. Static objects arranged in a diagonal composition appear to move. Tilting a stable horizontal world diagonally evokes a sense of disorientation and instability. Diagonal lines can be effective in adding tension to a scene.

Lines provide a visual pathway for the viewer's eye to follow. However, a line in a composition does not have to physically be a line. Implied lines come in all forms. These are often referred to as leading lines in scenes. When designing your composition, have something lead into the subject from near a bottom corner, like a road, path, fence, or line of trees to help the eye find the way to the center of interest.

They imply movement and direct the viewer's eye within a frame. Lines can be horizontal, vertical, or diagonal.

Shapes

Lines can also be connected to form shapes such as a triangle. A triangle is commonly used in compositions to frame action involving characters or objects. The dynamic nature of a triangle allows the audience to follow around the three points to create a sense of unity in the composition.

Triangular compositions communicate the roles of each character.

A courtroom scene is a good example of a triangular composition. The judge is positioned at the height of the triangle's apex making him superior to the lawyer and the witness testifying. If the triangle is reversed, with the apex at the bottom, the character positioned there appears much weaker than the other two. An interrogation scene in a crime drama is a good example.

Turning the triangle upside down conveys a different emotional response from the audience.

Lines can be curved to create circular compositions. The circle is a universal symbol signifying completeness, unity, perfection, and eternity. A circular composition draws the audience deeper into the shot. It provides a more intimate space for the audience.

No matter how you use lines or shapes, your composition needs to have one and only one center of interest. The audience needs to be attracted to that one point. In the previous examples, note the gaze of each character. They do not look out toward the audience but at the center of interest in the shot. Their gazes carry our eyes to what is important.

A circular composition draws the audience deeper into the shot.

Avoid Tangent Lines

Lines are strong design elements that direct the audience's attention and imply dynamic action. However, lines can also be distracting elements in a frame if used incorrectly. For example, if a line passes through the head of a character, it seems to cut into the head.

Overlapping lines are OK, but avoid connecting outlines of one form to another. The connection made is called a tangent and can be visually confusing to the eye. It joins the two forms as one when they need to be distinguished as two separate elements. To fix this, separate your objects or make sure there is no clear intersection of lines in the shot.

For more information on visual storytelling, read **Understanding Comics: The Invisible Art** by Scott McCloud.

Being Dominant

If all the elements in a shot are of equal size or shape, with nothing being clearly dominant, it becomes very difficult for the audience to know what to focus on. Often certain elements within a composition seem to leap off the screen and take visual precedence. Contrasting scale establishes dominance and creates visual harmony in a composition. Audiences naturally seek out the most dominant element in a composition.

Color

Color serves as a dominant element. It can separate one object from others to attract the audience's attention. You can also tap into a viewer's psychological interpretation of color. Your audience members will have different reactions to different colors. The color red is a good example; it can be perceived as meaning power, strength, or passion, but it can also be associated with anger, violence, or danger. Cultures share common opinions about color, for example:

- **Red**: hot, power, anger, violence, love, fire
- **Yellow**: warm, joyful, sickness
- **Blue**: cold, tranquil, peace, water, sadness
- **Orange**: courage, cheerful, energy
- **Green**: growth, healthy, greed, envy, good luck

For more information on visual storytelling, read **The Power of Visual Storytelling: How to Use Visuals, Videos, and Social Media to Market Your Brand** by Ekaterina Walter and Jessica Gioglio.

Color establishes dominance in the frame. It can be manipulated to reflect the mood of a scene and personality of its occupants.

Value

Value refers to the lightness and darkness of a color. Contrast between light and dark can also create compositional dominance in a scene. Every element within the frame has a specific brightness. By increasing the light in one area or on a subject you create an area of dominance within a composition. A bright object or area in a frame gives it extra weight and attracts the viewer's eye.

Areas of darkness can also serve as dominant compositional elements. The term film noir, French for "black film," refers to Hollywood crime dramas popular in the 1940s and '50s. Cinematographers in the Film Noir genre experimented with shadows in their shots. For them, black was the most important element.

Shapes and Forms

Forms can be very effective in telling a visual story. Having a character in shadow forces the audience to focus more on the figure's form, and less on the detail. If the character is gesturing, the resulting silhouetted image clearly communicates all the visual information the audience needs to know without losing them to any secondary details.

Cinematographers sometimes add forms and shapes to "frame" the focal point in the composition. This framing device can be anything from a rectangular doorway or window, to more organic shapes such as a tree branch that hangs into the shot. Using a frame within the frame breaks up the space in interesting ways. It also allows the audience to focus on two separate events in the same frame.

Getting into Character

When creating an animated story, one key element is the appeal of its characters. Characters come in all shapes and sizes. Creating a unique and compelling character often begins with a distinct look. What is your character going to look like? The answer is completely up to you. Character design is an art form unto itself. Let's look at some basic guidelines that, if used, will improve your character designs.

Casting the Characters

Before you start sketching out your characters, reread the story you have chosen to animate or make interactive. Answer the following questions that your audience will want to know:

- What is the character's physical body makeup?
- Two arms and two legs? Four legs? Eight tentacles?
- Does the character resemble a person, an animal, a plant, an object, or something no one has ever seen before?
- Is the character's body thin, overweight, muscular, or soft?
- Is the character tall, short, or hunched over?
- Is the character male, female, or something else?
- Does the character walk, slither, fly, or swim?
- What colors identify the character?
- What type of clothes does the character wear, if any?

After picturing the visual look, think about the character in regard to the "staging" of your visual story, ask yourself:

- Is the character the center of interest or merely a prop?
- How big is the character in relation to the other characters? The background? The props?
- Does the character animate? How much does the character move?
- Will the audience see the character from different angles?
- Does the character speak?

The goal is to design an appealing character for the audience.

Shaping Up

Simplify the design by building your characters out of basic shapes. Look at the world around you; you should be able to distinguish squares, rectangles, circles, ovals, and triangles present in almost everything you see. These shapes can also help the audience understand what type of character it is. Each shape subliminally conveys a different personality trait. The shapes you choose become the underlying structure for your character's makeup and personality.

Let's take a look at some character designs using basic shapes:

- **Squares and Rectangles:** Characters built primarily out of rectangles tend to be big, muscular jocks, superheroes, bullies, and military characters. Square and rectangular shapes suggest strength, dependability, and lack of intelligence, as in the phrase "blockhead."

- **Circles and Ovals:** Circular shapes are used for characters with small bodies, for example, children. A character constructed out of circular, round shapes appears soft, cuddly, and non-threatening.

- **Triangular Shapes:** Similar to rectangles, triangular shapes can be used for strong characters that have a chiseled jawbone structure or a really large neck. If the triangle is turned upside down, the resulting shape can be used for female characters or nerdy characters that lack self-confidence.

For more information on character design, read *Cartooning: The Ultimate Character Design Book* by Chris Hart.

Experiment with the basic shapes to determine which shape best suits your character design.

Basic Character Proportions

The average human adult is about six to eight heads tall. What does that mean? Use the character's head as a unit of measurement; stack a bunch of heads on top of each other. An adult human character would be six to eight of those heads tall including the head of the character.

The age and gender of your character determines how many heads tall the character should be. The unit of measurement doesn't change; it's always based on the height of your character's head. A child has a much smaller head ratio of about two to three. A mother is about five to seven heads tall.

Remember that this is a general rule for characters that mimic human proportions. If you are creating more of a caricature, you do not need to fit the character exactly within these dimensions but it does give you a starting point that you can use.

Use the character's head as a unit of measurement.

Chapter 9 | Understanding Visual Storytelling

Contrasting Characters

If you are building more than one character, keep in mind that they all need to live together in the same environment. In order to get along, all characters should share a fairly similar visual style. A good way to see this is to line them all up next to one another. Make a size comparison chart that show's each character's size relative to the other characters in the story. The end result looks something like a police lineup.

Having a similar visual style does not mean that you have to forego contrast. There is truth in the saying, "Opposites attract." If all your characters shared the same physical build with the only difference in design being clothes, who would you focus on more? Audiences need to be intrigued by your character's individuality and contrast is a good method to use.

Two characters that contrast well against each other are always more interesting than two characters who are exactly the same. Stories have at least two characters, or two sides to a character. Think about popular cartoon duos: Tom and Jerry, Yogi Bear and Boo Boo, Snoopy and Woodstock. These characters differ in physical height, build, and color.

Create a character size comparison chart to make sure they all share the same visual style.

Using Color

Let's focus on color. Certain colors communicate information about a character. It is generally accepted that red can be passionate and sometimes dangerous. Blue is cold and masculine, while a lighter shade can be perceived as feminine. Yellow conveys a sense of being cheerful, bright, and it is eye catching.

The color green symbolizes healthy and alive. Purple is associated with royalty. Orange is warm and inviting. Neutral grays are rather dark and mysterious. The color brown is considered earthy and old. Be aware of these color connotations in designing your characters because the audience will pick up on their meanings subconsciously.

What about black? To make sure your character stands out in the crowd fill in its outline using black. Only using positive and negative space removes all detail except the defining outline of the character. A memorable character can be reduced to a silhouette, and still be immediately recognizable.

For more information on character design, read *Creating Characters with Personality: For Film, TV, Animation, Video Games, and Graphic Novels* by Tom Bancroft and Glen Keane.

German filmmaker *Lotte Reiniger* is a pioneer in silhouette animation. Her 65-minute film *Die Abenteuer des Prinzen Achmed* (The Adventures of Prince Achmed) is widely considered to be the world's first animated feature.

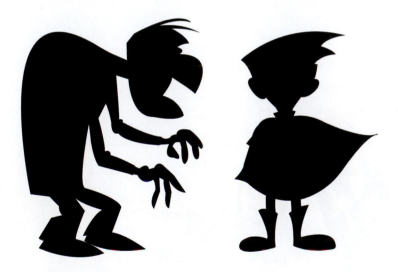

Thinking Like a Cinematographer

A cinematographer looks though the camera viewfinder to frame a shot. The three most common camera shots are the long shot, medium shot, and close-up. Of course, films are not made up of these three camera shots alone. The long shot and close-up can also have extremes that can visually heighten the drama and tension in a story. Keep in mind that these shots do not refer to the actual distance between the camera and the subject, but to the relative size of the subject in the viewfinder.

- An **extreme long shot** (ELS) shows the vastness of an area or setting. It is typically used to frame the setting at the beginning or ending of a story. This can be an effective visual tool in generating an emotional response from your audience. For example, if a character is lost in the desert, an extreme long shot would not only amplify the desert's grand scale but the character's isolation from civilization.

- A **long shot** (LS) is used to frame the action. This shot shows the place, the characters, and the action. Examples of a long shot include action that takes place in a room, on a street, outside a house, or under a tree. A character is shown complete from head to toe, occupying about one-third of the height of the frame.

An extreme long shot not only shows the setting for your story, but provides an emotional response from the audience.

- A **medium shot** (MS) frames the characters from the waist or knees up. The character's gestures and facial expressions are shown with just enough background to establish the setting. It is the most common shot used in film and television. It draws the audience in closer, making the story more personal for them. Often this shot is used when characters are speaking to one another.

- In a **close-up** (CU), a character's head and shoulders are shown. This shot invites the audience to become a participant in the story by visually coming face-to-face with the characters. They can see and hopefully feel the emotions of the character.

- For more dramatic effect, use an **extreme close-up** (ECU). This shot focuses the audience's attention on whatever is significant in the shot or facial reaction of a character. A close-up or extreme close-up doesn't always have to frame emotion. Close-ups can also reveal private information to the audience or emphasize symbols within the shot.

Do you always have to see these camera shots in this order? No. Determine the order of the shots that best serves your story.

Like a painter, the way in which you frame the space has a direct effect on your audience. Always try to introduce variety by using different types of camera shots. The goal is to move from one shot to another without the audience becoming confused or lost. Select a camera shot appropriate for the action. Then determine the order of the shots that best serves the dramatic needs of your story.

LONG SHOT
Frame the Scene

MEDIUM SHOT
Frame the Action

CLOSE-UP
Frame the Emotion

Camera shots play an important role in visual storytelling. Each shot provides a visual step closer for the audience to take and become fully involved with the story. Equally important to the relative size of the subject in the shot is the camera's point of view or angle. Not all shots are taken at eye level.

Chapter 9 | Understanding Visual Storytelling

Camera Angles

A carefully chosen camera angle can heighten the drama of the story. It is the camera angle that makes a shot dynamic. Positioning the camera determines the point of view from which the audience will see the shot. Each time the camera is moved, it transports the audience to a new point of view. That's why every change in camera angle should be carefully planned.

- In a **high-angle shot**, the camera is placed above the horizon line tilted down to view the subject. This camera angle can be used in conjunction with an extreme long shot to frame an aesthetically pleasing landscape. If combined with a medium shot, the high angle can create a sense of insignificance or vulnerability in the character shown. The character appears weak and defenseless.

- In a **low-angle shot**, the camera is tilted up to view the subject. This camera angle creates a sense of awe and superiority. Strong characters shown from a low angle seem to have more power as they dominate the frame.

- For a **Dutch-angle shot**, the vertical axis of the camera is at an angle to the vertical axis of the subject. It creates a sense of being off balanced or insecure. Often evil characters or characters in dangerous situations are shown through a tilted angle.

- A **bird's-eye view** takes the high-angle shot to the extreme. The camera is positioned directly overhead.

For information on cinematography, read *The Five C's of Cinematography: Motion Picture Filming Techniques* by Joseph V. Mascelli.

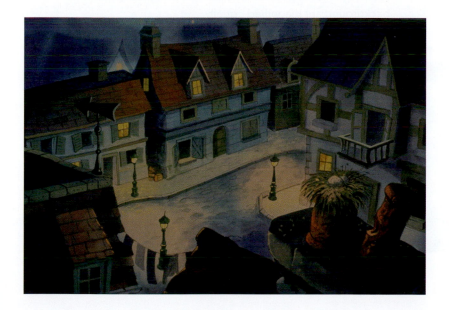

Examples of the bird's-eye view in film include looking down on buildings in a city or following a car driving on a road.

Camera Movements

Shots can also be defined by the movement of the camera. Camera movements are used to focus the audience's attention and involve them in the scene they are watching. Let's discuss some common camera movements used in film.

- A **pan** (P) shot rotates the camera horizontally from left to right or right to left, similar to moving your head from side to side. Pans are used for establishing shots, where the camera pans across the horizon of a landscape. A pan can also give the feeling of searching for something within in a shot.

- A **tilt** (T) is a pan in the vertical direction, up or down. It is most commonly used to reveal a tall building or a person. It can be a very effective visual storytelling technique if used properly. For example, tilting up from a character's feet to their head creates added tension as the audience anticipates what the character's face will look like.

- Cameras can also travel from one place to another within a single shot. This is called a **tracking shot** (TS). The camera tracks or follows along with the subject. In some tracking shots, both the camera and the character move. A tracking shot can also be applied when the subject matter stays in one place and the camera moves in relation to it. The camera can move forward, called a **truck in**, or backward, called a **truck out**.

- **Zooming** is an optical effect that magnifies the image. Perspective is not affected because the foreground and background are magnified equally.

A panning shot is typically used to establish a location or setting for the story.

  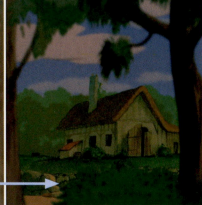

Using the 180-Degree Rule

A scene showing two people having dinner in a restaurant might consist of three basic shots: a medium shot showing both of them seated at the table and two close-ups, one for each person. These shots orient the viewer to the space and how the characters occupy it. In order to shoot the scene and edit each shot together effectively, it is important to understand the 180-degree rule.

The **line of action** is an imaginary line that determines the direction your characters and objects face when viewed through your camera. When you cross the line of action, you reverse the screen direction of everything captured through the camera, even though the characters or object have not moved an inch.

The image below illustrates this concept using the two characters seen from an overhead view. The imaginary line runs through both characters' heads. Its direction is based on how the characters face one another. The primary rule is to pick one side of the line and stay on it throughout the scene. This is called the **180-degree rule**.

TOP VIEW

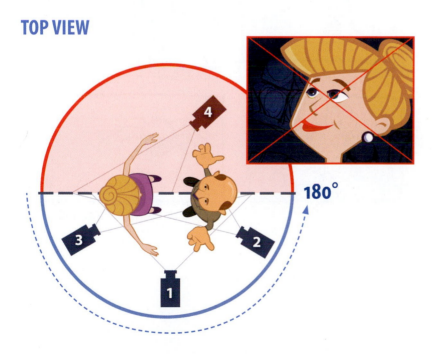

180°

As long as the camera stays on the front side of the line, the man will be looking screen left and the woman will be looking screen right. If you cross the line, they'll be looking in the opposite directions, although they haven't moved at all. You can choose from a variety of camera shots and angles as long as you stay on one side of the 180-degree line.

Chapter Case Study:
Illustrating the Space with Storyboards

As a visual storyteller, you do not write a script, you draw it. Start applying the camera techniques you just learned by drawing rough thumbnail sketches. On a sheet of paper, sketch out camera shots that you think would be effective in illustrating your story. You don't have to draw well to create a thumbnail board so don't spend a lot of time fine-tuning your art.

The purpose of a thumbnail board is to quickly determine the layout of your shots, not highlight your illustration skills. Even though the artwork is rough, the thumbnails should still clearly define which characters are in a shot, the camera's position, and the direction of motion, if any. List details underneath each sketch as notes to clarify what you envision. This can include anything from sound effects to special effects. Creating rough thumbnails first help you organize your animation layout and provide a visual format to build your storyboard.

For information on storyboarding, read *Storyboard Design Course: Principles, Practice, and Techniques* by Giuseppe Cristiano.

When visualizing your story, start with a series of rough thumbnail sketches.

Chapter 9 | Understanding Visual Storytelling

What Is a Storyboard?

A **storyboard** is a production tool that illustrates a story shot-by-shot using a series of sequential images. In film, it allows the director to plan the camera shots, the camera angles, and the camera movement to produce a cohesive and entertaining story to the audience. When finished, your storyboard will become a blueprint for all the important shots that will be in the final animation. In visual form it looks like a comic strip.

  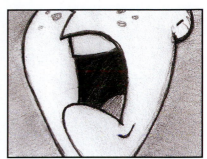

The Walt Disney Studios developed the storyboarding process in the 1930s for its animated films. Storyboarding is still used in Hollywood today as a visual tool to lay out a movie, one sketch for each shot or scene. These sketches show the layout of the shot and provide information about what is happening and how the shot fits in the movie.

A storyboard should visually answer the following questions:

- Which characters are in the frame, and how are they moving?
- What are the characters saying to each other, if anything?
- Where is the "camera" positioned? Is the camera moving?

Storyboards illustrate a story shot-by-shot. A feature-length animation can contain hundreds, if not thousands, of shots. A storyboard becomes the blueprint for all the important shots that produce a cohesive story for the audience.

Storyboard Assignment

For this chapter case study, let's apply the cinematic techniques discussed so far to design a storyboard for the popular nursery rhyme, *Little Miss Muffet*. The rhyme contains all the necessary storytelling ingredients. Little Miss Muffet is the protagonist whose goal is to eat her curds and whey. The villain, or antagonist, is the spider. The climax occurs when the spider drops in to visit our heroine. This action results in scaring Miss Muffet away – the resolution to the story.

PART 1: Breaking Down the Story Visually

Each line in the nursery rhyme can be conveniently broken down into a manageable shot. There are a lot of ways to visually show this story. For this example, let's follow a traditional cinematic approach that many filmmakers might use.

Visual storytelling treatment for the *Little Miss Muffet* nursery rhyme.

Nursery Rhyme Line	Camera	Rationale
Little Miss Muffet	ELS	Establishing shot
Sat on a tuffet,	LS	Frame the action
Eating her curds and whey;	MS	Frame the protagonist
Along came a spider,	Tilt/MS	Frame the antagonist
Who sat down beside her	CU	Face-to-face with the audience
And frightened...	ECU	Frame the emotion
Miss Muffet away	ELS	Re-establish the setting

PART 2: Drawing the Storyboard Panels

Drawing on paper is still an effective way to build storyboards. Each drawn panel should show the basic shot layout, character gestures, and camera placement. There are no exercise files to download for this chapter. You can follow along with the examples shown or experiment and create your own illustrations.

For information on storyboarding, read ***Directing the Story: Professional Storytelling and Storyboarding Techniques for Live Action and Animation*** by Francis Glebas.

The opening shot establishes the setting for where the story takes place using an extreme long shot (ELS). This shot clearly outlines for the audience the setting, the tree on the hill, and the main character. This can be referred to as an **establishing shot**, or if the story takes place in only one location as this one does, a master shot.

The opening shot establishing the setting for where the story takes place.

To draw the audience in slowly, the camera tracks in to a long shot that frames the action. When storyboarding the camera movements, use arrows to indicate direction. Arrows can drastically save time by indicating a single movement without you having to drawing multiple frames.

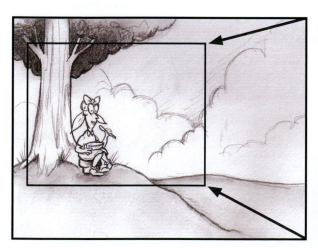

The next shot is a medium shot that shows Miss Muffet from the waist up. This shot provides enough space to capture her physical body gestures and her facial reactions as she enjoys eating her food. The audience sees how the main character feels at that particular moment in the story.

The medium shot frames the character's body gestures and expressions.

This medium shot of Miss Muffet continues until the camera's point of view changes. The camera tilts up vertically and tracks in to reveal the spider slowly descending. The camera angle used is a low-angle shot to make the spider appear more menacing. Arrows are used to indicate the vertical tilt in camera direction, the movement of the spider, and the minor camera tracking used to focus the audience's attention on the spider.

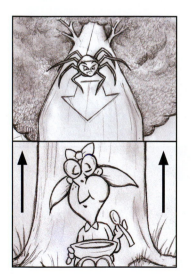

After the spider moves out of the frame, a close-up shot is used to show the spider's body and its proximity to Miss Muffet's face. The close-up primarily focuses on the main character's face. The camera angle is at eye level, putting the audience face-to-face with the villain and equal to Miss Muffet's point of view.

When our heroine becomes aware of her little friend, an extreme close-up highlights the terror. Many horror films make use of extreme close-ups, especially zeroing in on a character's eyes to convey fear. This type of shot is great for adding a dramatic punch, or emphasis to the action in the story.

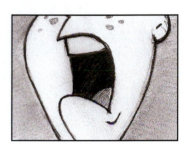

The last shot provides closure by reestablishing the extreme long shot shown at the beginning. This shot also clearly illustrates how the setting has been altered by the events of the story with our heroine running away. This is one way to show this story. Experiment with different camera shots in a different order to see how it affects the narrative.

The last camera shot provides closure to the story. It also clearly illustrates how the setting has been altered by the events of the story with our heroine running away.

Summary

A good story is judged by the emotional impact it has on its audience. Understanding its structure is a key factor in making your stories great. Most animation begins with the development of a story.

Composition is the structure behind your shot. Its function is to direct the audience's attention to what is happening in the scene. Design elements such as line, shape, color, and value are used together to form a composition. Lines direct the audience's attention and imply dynamic action. Color can be manipulated to reflect the mood of a scene and the personality of its occupants.

Once you have determined your story and its visual style, the next step in the production process is to develop a storyboard. Storyboards illustrate a story shot-by-shot. A feature-length animation can contain hundreds, if not thousands, of shots. A storyboard becomes the blueprint for all the important shots that produce a cohesive and entertaining story for the audience.

This completes the chapter on visual storytelling. You should now be able to:

- Describe the components that make up a good story.
- Build a composition that keeps the audience visually interested in a story.
- Discuss how lines, shapes, colors, and values are used together to form a composition.
- Create unique and compelling characters for animation.
- Use different camera shots to "show" the story.
- Apply visual storytelling techniques to create a storyboard for a short animation.

The next, and last, chapter focuses on usability testing.

10

Evaluating and Testing Usability

Usability testing is one of the most important steps in evaluating user-centered interaction for digital design. The goal is to identify any usability problems, collect qualitative and quantitative data, and determine the user's satisfaction with the experience. As well as evaluating technical issues that may occur.

This chapter provides an overview of the content and methods for usability testing. Upon the completion of this chapter, you will be able to:

- Describe the need for usability testing.
- Develop a usability study plan.
- Determine which metrics to evaluate.

Why Usability Testing?

Usability evaluation and testing serve to improve the interactive user experience with digital products such as websites, mobile apps, and other digital interactive experiences. It also helps to reduce both development time and costs. It is an inspection method used to identify usability problems in both the user interface (UI) and interaction (IxD) design.

The goal is to determine if a target user understands the purpose and functionality of a digital product and can successfully interact with it. Any additional desired features that could enhance the overall user experience are also discovered. Finally, testing highlights content issues such as providing the right level, organization, and flow of information presented.

When to Test?

Testing early and often is the most important aspect of usability testing during your digital design cycle. Testing early and throughout the process will assist in identifying any user issues early on. As described in previous chapters, wireframes and prototypes are key in the design development stage. Testing is essential in delivering a successful user experience.

Traditionally, usability testing was reserved for the very end of the production cycle. As a result, the research and documentation process ended up consuming an enormous amount of time creating longer design and development periods before a digital product was released. This is often referred to as the **Waterfall** model due to its linear process in which progress flows downward sequentially, like an actual waterfall.

Crowdsourcing for Usability Testing

by Di Liu, Randolph G Bias, Matthew Lease, and Rebecca Kuipers

"Beautiful designs do not automatically mean they are good user experiences."

– Andy Pratt & Jason Nunes

WATERFALL MODEL

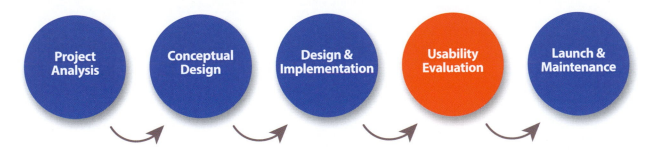

Another model, referred to as **Lean UX**, focuses on the actual experience being designed. Traditional research documentation is stripped down to its bare components to reduce preproduction time and get started with actual design and implementation. Digital products have very short, iterative cycles using low-fidelity prototypes. This model also includes all members of the business and implementation team (designers and developers) collaborating together to create a successful experience.

Even though the Lean UX model focuses on eliminating waste through limited documentation, it is still data driven. Its goal is to test everything to make sure the designers and developers understand the customer's needs and problems. It validates the digital design cycle at each stage.

Lean UX by Jeff Gothelf and Josh Seiden is a good resource for learning about the Lean UX model.

LEAN UX MODEL

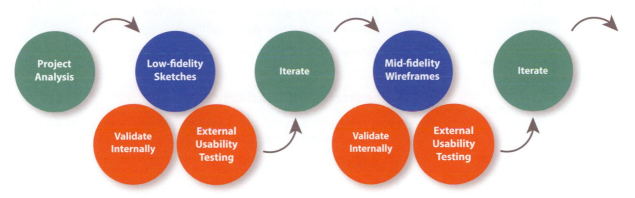

As for the user interface design, keep it simple. It should be easy to learn, and should support the users' goals and tasks. Don't make the interface confusing, because an intuitive and simple design is far more appealing. A satisfying and engaging experience is the key to a successful user interface. Part of usability testing should include a heuristic evaluation. **Heuristics** provides a set of guidelines for an evaluator to follow when reviewing and assessing a user interface design. This concept was made popular by Jakob Nielsen.

The Nielsen Norman Group provides many articles on their research and evaluations of user interface designs at *www.nngroup.com*.

Whitney Quesenbery's
5 Dimensions of Usability

Effective – how completely and accurately the work or experience is completed or goals reached

Efficient – how quickly this work can be completed

Engaging – how well the interface draws the user into the interaction and how pleasant and satisfying it is to use

Error Tolerant – how well the product prevents errors and can help the user recover from mistakes that do occur

Easy to Learn – how well the product supports both the initial orientation and continued learning throughout the complete lifetime of use

Jakob Nielsen's Definition of Usability

Jakob Nielsen is a web usability consultant and has been called "the guru of webpage usability" (*The New York Times*). He is cofounder of the Nielsen Norman Group. Their website, *www.nngroup.com*, is dedicated to usability research. Jakob Nielsen defines several properties that produce effective usability for websites and app design. These include:

- **Learnability**: How easy is it for users to accomplish basic tasks the first time they encounter the design?

- **Efficiency**: Once users have learned the design, how quickly can they perform tasks?

- **Memorability**: When users return to the design after a period of not using it, how easily can they reestablish proficiency?

- **Errors**: How many errors do users make, how severe are these errors, and how easily can they recover from the errors?

- **Satisfaction**: How pleasant is it to use the design?

Getting Started with Usability Testing

Usability testing consists of target users trying to complete typical tasks while observers watch, listen, and take notes. When planning a test:

- Define your usability goals

- Know what to measure; identify tasks to be completed

- Consider competitive testing (compare your site/app to others as part of the testing)

- Set expectations for time allocation

- Decide on the type of responses to consider in testing:
  ◊ Verbal Response
  ◊ Multiple Choice
  ◊ Rating Scale
  ◊ Written Response

- Focus on the users' needs, goals, and tasks
  ◊ Are they able to complete a task?
  ◊ How much effort was required to complete the task?
  ◊ Were the users' expectations met?

- Identify usability metrics to evaluate

- Determine how and when to evaluate the results

Qualitative and quantitative data will help you to understand what problems exist, how many, and why.

- **Qualitative** – Why / When / What
- **Quantitative** – How many

Iterative Testing with Targeted Users

Recommended testing intervals include starting with evaluating competitor or similar products through the final deliverable:

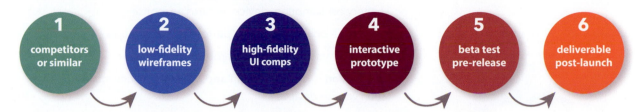

| 1 competitors or similar | 2 low-fidelity wireframes | 3 high-fidelity UI comps | 4 interactive prototype | 5 beta test pre-release | 6 deliverable post-launch |

Testing Methods & Tools

There are various methods of testing. Here are just a few:

- Hand-drawn sketches show your concept for preliminary feedback.
- Use a software tool that would provide statistics based on the wireframes and designs submitted.
- Hire a third-party usability team that specializes in this field.
- Submit your design and wireframes to an external evaluator to obtain feedback.

Pick the right tool that helps communicate the design concept. The goal is to explain complex problems in a simple way and test if they're clear and meaningful to people. Throughout the design process, usability testing methods to obtain user feedback might include:

- Participatory Design
- Paper Prototyping
- Video Prototyping
- Walk-through, Surveys
- Focus Groups
- Heuristic Evaluation
- Quality Assurance

Data can come from observations including audio/video recordings, surveys, and interviews.

A helpful website is *www.usability.gov/how-to-and-tools/methods/index.html.*

In addition to the visual design, test the overall performance. Make sure your design is optimized for the intended device and that all links work correctly.

Types of testing for apps:

- **Usability** – overall function and user experience satisfaction
- **Interface** – testing of buttons, navigation flow, menu option, external links to social media
- **Compatibility** – operating system versions, mobile browsing, screen sizes, various devices
- **Operational Testing** – back-up, save, and recovery plan, data loss, behavior interaction with other device functions
- **Performance** – memory, loading, connection speed, response time, battery consumption, device features' response
- **Services** – online and offline performance of an app
- **Security** – validation of data protection
- **Installation** – validation of an app by installing/uninstalling it on various devices
- **Low-level Resource** – memory usage, auto deletion of temporary files, local database growth

Types of testing for websites:

- **Usability** – navigation, content, help features
- **Interface** – user interface of servers and database
- **Functionality** – links, connections, forms
- **Compatibility** – operating systems, mobile browsing, printing, browser compatibility
- **Performance** – memory, loading, speed, stress test
- **Security** – validation of data protection

Tools to assist in testing:

- Monitoring tools
- Task-based tools
- Heatmap/Eye Tracking/User movement recording
- Feedback/Survey
- User recruiting sites

Eye tracking and heatmaps show how much a user has looked at certain parts of the screen. Where the user looks the most is colored red in heatmaps. There are many other usability testing tools that are a fraction of the cost of traditional testing tools and can give you results that are close to traditional usability testing facility results.

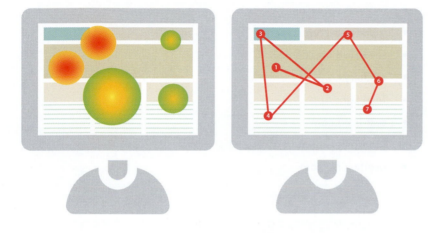

Test how the user interacts with the content and how the system responds to the user's actions in a timely manner.

INPUT

FEEDBACK

ERRORS

DEVICE

TIME

Online resources and software provide an overall good simulation of how your design will work on a device. Ideally, you want to test on the device itself for optimum usability testing.

When it comes to testing your digital design, there are numerous resources available that simulate mobile devices. Here is sampling of some of the software available for testing an app and/or website:

- Google Play Native App Beta Testing
- hockeyapp.net
- mobilephoneemulator.com
- ready.mobi (mobiready)
- responsivepx.com
- quirktools.com/screenfly
- silverbackapp.com
- testfairy.com
- TestFlight App
- testdroid.com
- ubertesters.com
- usertesting.com

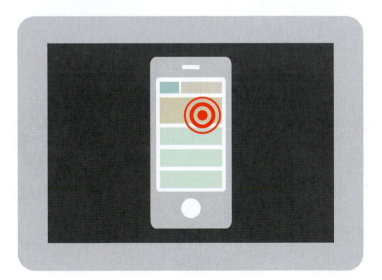

Usability Test Procedure

Here is one example outline of a testing plan:

Define the Testing Audience

- Recruit test participants
- Select observers and moderators if needed

Develop the Test Plan

- Identify the goal(s) of the test
- Identify the tasks/scenarios/functions to be tested

Set Up the Testing Environment

- Software installed
- Physical space
- Recording devices: audio, video, and/or photo

Conduct the Usability Test

- Prepare the test materials
  - ◊ Physical space
  - ◊ Questionnaires or similar
- Conduct test sessions
  - ◊ User has a series of tasks to complete
  - ◊ Observer documents the actions of the user (and only intervenes as a last resort)

Process Steps for Prototyping Review

When developing your prototype, evaluation and testing are on-going throughout the process:

- Research
- Planning
- Content requirements
- Design ideation and brainstorming
- Information architecture
- Sketching concepts
- Wireframes
- Evaluation and testing iteration
- Mockups
- Evaluation and testing iteration
- Prototyping
- Evaluation and testing iteration
- Development

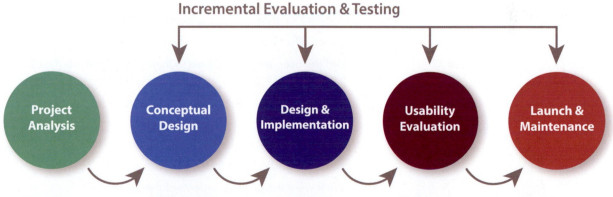

- Debrief the participants and observers
  - ◊ Follow up on any specific problems that occurred

Usability Test Results Analysis

- Analyze data and observations
- Report findings and recommendations

Chapter Case Study:
Usability Study and Assessment

Usability studies inform design and development teams on whether their product is understandable and usable enough for final delivery. Their goal is to identify revisions and areas for improvement in the functionality and communication of information. It is common practice that the entire team observe the target users throughout the entire usability test.

The test typically consists of three parts:

- **Prep the participant:** Review what the usability test will include and put the users at ease by asking information about their background, interests, etc. This can take anywhere from 5 to 10 minutes.
- **Administer scenario-based tasks:** Ask the users to complete specific tasks with the prototype. Allocate at least 30 minutes for this part.
- **Conduct a wrap-up interview:** Ask the participants about their overall impressions and feelings about the product. This can take anywhere from 10 to 20 minutes.

The data collected should answer the following:

- Was the user successful in completing the task?
- How much effort was required to complete the task?
  - ◊ Did the user understand how to interact with the interface?
  - ◊ Did the user make any errors? If so, did the error prevention help get the user back on task? How frequently did the user make mistakes?
  - ◊ How long did it take for the user to complete the task?
- Was the user satisfied with the overall user experience?
  - ◊ What were the positive aspects of the prototype?
  - ◊ What are areas for improvement in the functionality?

Usability studies determine if a product's user interface and functionality needs to be fixed or improved before final delivery.

Did the user complete the task?

Did the user make any mistakes?

How long did it take them?

How do they feel about it?

Based on the analysis of the data collected, the team needs to identify the overall user satisfaction in relation to the following:

- **User Experience Design:** Did the participants like using the product and would they recommend it to others?

- **Navigation and Orientation:** Did they understand how to get to the content and know where they were once immersed in it?

- **Content:** Was the information relevant to their needs?

There are no exercise files to download for this chapter. You can follow along with the example shown. The following project was designed by Jordan Reading, a graduate student in the MFA Visual Communication Design program at the Rochester Institute of Technology.

The title of Jordan's project is **ROC DOX**. The goal of the product was to provide new and current Rochester Institute of Technology students with the resources to help them maintain their health while at school. Students tend to put off preventive care due to not knowing where they should go off-campus for care, or how they will get there – especially when they are new to the area. This mobile application provided a hub to manage all doctor appointments and medical information such as appointments, and insurance information.

The objectives of the ROC DOX mobile application was to motivate college students to maintain and receive regular health check-ups through fast and easy doctor research.

Low-Fidelity Wireframe Testing

Jordan designed her wireframes to determine the user flow in searching for a new doctor and scheduling an appointment. She conducted a usability study with six target users. The results highlighted the strengths in the user interface design and some content issues to fix:

Dashboard · Search Results · Search Filters · Doctor Details · Appointment · Confirm

Annotations

1. Dashboard provides upcoming appointment reminders
2. Swipe-down access to filters
3. Search service sections (i.e., doctor, hospitals, etc.)
4. Drop-down specialty menu to filter doctors
5. Slider functions to change distance values

6. Map indicates where office is and available transportation
7. Displays available appointments; swipe allows for scheduling
8. Displays current month calendar; swipe for additional months
9. Animated check-mark confirms that the appointment was made

❌ **Section navigation at the bottom of the screen is not noticed right away.**

Solution
Relocate this navigation menu toward the top of the screen to ensure it's seen immediately.

✅ **Overview of doctor listing that is displayed directly in the search results.**

❌ **Too much information.**
Feels over-whelming and the type is overall too small.

Solution
Group the information into more visually similar chunks to allow for better communication.

✅ **Easier access to the soonest available appointments.**
Needs to have a confirmation screen after the appointment button has been pressed.

High-Fidelity Wireframe Testing

Jordan's next iteration was a set of high-fidelity wireframes with the actual content added to the user interface design. She conducted another usability study with the same six target users. For this study, she recorded the participants using her smartphone to review at a later time.

The results highlighted the strengths in the user interface design and some issues with button labeling to fix for the next iterative design stage:

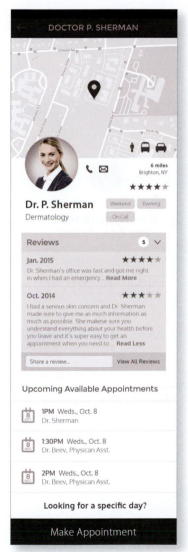

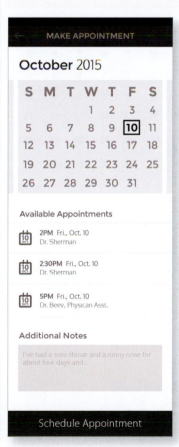

✅ **Reviews are available up-front and it is easy to access various available routes to the office.**

❌ **Found the "Make Appointment" button confusing and intimidating.** Terminology sounded committal and didn't invite the user to search for other available appointments.

Solution
Replace the term "Make" with "Browse" to communicate the idea of seeking out additional available appointments.

✅ **Easy to learn the gesture of swiping from left to right to navigate through the months in the calendar.**

Interactive Prototype Testing

Jordan's next iteration was to build an interactive prototype using **Proto.io**. This online prototyping tool allows designers to create fully interactive high-fidelity prototypes that look and work as close as possible to the final mobile application. For this study, Jordan was looking to see if any additional features were desired by the users. She video recorded the usability tests with her target users to review at a later time.

A helpful website for high-fidelity prototyping is at *proto.io.*

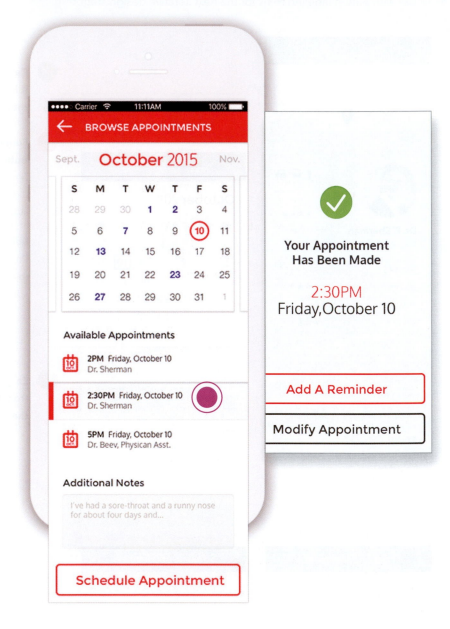

It's All About the User's Experience

Remember, whether you are designing for desktop, mobile, or wearable devices, you should focus on a "user-centered design." Design is about satisfying the user's needs and solving their problems. A user may be one individual or thousands, all with the same wants and needs.

Designing for multiple screens and devices poses unique challenges. Designers need to take a holistic approach to understanding the users, their tasks, and their environments. The goal of usability testing is to identify any usability problems, collect qualitative and quantitative data, and determine the user's satisfaction with the experience.

As a review from Chapter 1, designers have to understand the following about the intended users:

Audience: Age? Gender? Location? Income Levels? Education? Disabilities?

Environment: Home? Work? On-the-go? Noisy or quiet space? Outdoors or indoors?

Time: Leisure? Budgeted/time allotted? Quick check?

Device: Old? New? Bandwidth Issues? Connectivity Speeds?

Summary

Usability evaluation and testing enable you to identify the positive and negative aspects of an interactive experience. Testing throughout the process will result in a more efficient, engaging, and satisfying experience for the users.

Key principles from this chapter:

- Test early and test often.
- Investigate various testing methods.
- Utilize available tools and resources to assist in testing.

This completes the chapter. You should now be able to:

- Describe the purpose of usability testing.
- Develop a testing plan.
- Determine what metrics to evaluate.

Index